Tideline

by Wajdi Mouawad

Translated by Shelley Tepperman

Tideline

(Littoral)

Wajdi Mouawad

Translated from the French by
Shelley Tepperman

Playwrights Canada Press
Toronto • Canada

First published in French as *Littoral* by Leméac Éditeur Inc., Montreal.

Playwrights Canada Press
54 Wolseley St., 2nd fl. Toronto, Ontario CANADA M5T 1A5
416-703-0013 fax 416-703-0059
orders@playwrightscanada.com • www.playwrightscanada.com

Playwrights Canada Press acknowledges the support of the taxpayers of Canada and the province of Ontario through The Canada Council for the Arts and the Ontario Arts Council.

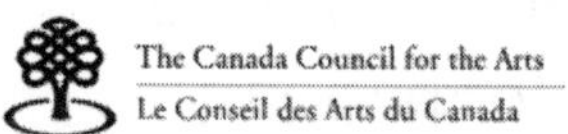

Cover art by Lino. Production Editor: Jodi Armstrong

National Library of Canada Cataloguing in Publication Data

Mouawad, Wajdi, 1968-
[Littoral. English]
Tideline

Translation of: Littoral.
ISBN 0-88754-633-1

I. Tepperman, Shelley II. Title. III. Title: Littoral. English.

PS8576.O87L5813 2002 C842'.54 C2001-903810-0
PQ3919.2.M665L5813 2002

First edition: July 2002.
Printed and bound by AGMV Marquis at Quebec, Canada.

We are nothing
What we seek is everything.
Holderlin, *Hyperion*

For Steve, Gilles, Isabelle,
For David, Pascal, Miro,
For Claude, Mathieu, Lucie,
For Charlotte, Michel, Robert,

For Manon, infinitely for Manon!

Wajdi Mouawad

Also for Anna.
Also for the other
The other is you.
Together and together
Greet the dawn.

Isabelle Leblanc

PLAYWRIGHT'S ACKNOWLEDGEMENTS

My infinite thanks to all those who, from near or far, contributed to the production of this work. I am particularly thinking of the National Theatre School of Canada, the Théâtre d'Aujourd'hui, the Theatre Festival of the Americas, the Théâtre Il va sans dire, of Magalie Amyot, of Isabelle Brodeur, of Eric Champoux, of Michèle Laliberté, of Pascal Sanchez, and of all of Mathieu's friends who loaned their musical instruments, and of all the friends and all those who we can't name here because it would take another book, all those who didn't count their time because their eyes were open.

TRANSLATOR'S ACKNOWLEDGEMENTS

Tideline has not yet been produced in English, so the comments of friends and colleagues have been especially valuable.

I am indebted to all those who read all or part of the manuscript, offered feedback and let me bounce ideas off them. Paul Lefebvre and Maryse Warda helped elucidate portions of the French text; Elaine Kennedy, Alon Nashman and Peter Hinton were generous with their insights and suggestions.

Thanks to Paula Danckert and Playwrights' Workshop Montreal for the stimulating dramaturgical dialogue and for providing a reading with actors. And to the actors who read the translation aloud and shared their thoughts and responses.

Special thanks especially to Soraya Peerbaye, long-distance companion on this journey, who read every word of every draft and offered thoughtful and critical comments at every stage.

Thanks to the Writing and Publication Section of The Canada Council for the Arts for their continued support for translations, and to Angela Rebeiro of Playwrights Canada Press for her commitment to publishing translations and supporting translators.

ON HOW THE WRITING BEGAN

Before everything there was encounter.

Isabelle Leblanc and I, sitting in Isabelle's apartment, in the kitchen, around a bottle of champagne, because we hadn't talked for far too long. Or seen each other. Or even *looked* at each other.

There was, before anything else, a young woman who was kind of fed up, sitting across from a guy who was kind of lost. Between them, (just beside the now half-empty bottle,) a thirst for ideas. That is, the desire to extricate ourselves from a world that was trying too hard to make us believe that intelligence was a waste of time, thinking a luxury, ideas a dead end.

So, here were two people, sitting across from each other, with an unquenchable thirst for the infinite, the same thirst shared by Lautréamont's dogs.[1]

Then there were actors and designers, friends, people we loved, who amazed us, sitting around a table. Around a question: "Here we are, we've just reached our thirties. What are we afraid of?"

Exploring that question, each one of us in turn trying to articulate our thoughts, trying to name what was lurking deep in our souls, allowed us to put our collective finger on certain essential things. We talked of love, of joy, of sorrow, of pain, of death. We also realized that while we were afraid of loving, we weren't afraid of dying, because our fear around death had to do with our parents, in the sense that we were not so much afraid of our own deaths as we were of the deaths of those who had given us life, and guided us through life; not only our birth parents, but also those who had parented us in our art.

During these exchanges, I started to develop an idea for a play, born of my readings of *Oedipus*, *Hamlet*, and *The Idiot*. Re-reading these works I realized what connected these three giants. Not only were all three princes (Prince of Thebes, Prince of Denmark, and Prince Mychkine), but beyond that, all three were deeply affected by their relationships with their fathers. One has killed his father, the other must avenge the murder of his father, and the third never knew his father. Finally, it seemed clear that these three characters were, in a way, telling different parts of the same story, one picking up where the other had left off.

If Oedipus suffers from blindness, Mychkine, his opposite, is the epitome of clear-sightedness; Hamlet, struggling between consciousness and the unconscious, is somewhere in between. And so the idea was born of a play depicting a character who, having lost his father, seeks a place to lay him to rest; during his quest he would meet three boys who were each, for me, a reflection of the three giants. Now, if Wilfrid is the reflection of my "lostness," Simone is the reflection of Isabelle's disillusionment. And in my eyes, it is significant that the first flesh and blood character Wilfrid meets is Simone, who was beautifully portrayed in the original production by Isabelle. It is also significant that the character of Joséphine, whose vocation is to bear the memory of the vanquished, is the last person Wilfrid meets. Because if Wilfrid belongs more to my world and Simone to Isabelle's, Joséphine is the perfect marriage between the two; Isabelle came up with the fabulous idea of the telephone books she carries, and I found its dramaturgical *raison d'être*, through the war and making them the weight that will anchor the father beneath the waves.

From that moment on, the way seemed clear: a man seeks a place to bury his father's remains; he returns to his ancestral land where meaningful encounters allow him to re-discover the very foundation of his existence and his identity. Then, the writing got underway, thirstily, almost a hallucination, with a life of its own. I must shout my thanks to the actors and designers who followed me through my writer and director's labyrinth with humour and discipline (and without keeping track of their hours); I'm enriched by their generosity.

Littoral (*Tideline*) was first and foremost born of an encounter and its meaning was born through encounters. That is, the terrible need to get outside of ourselves by letting the other burst into our lives, and the need to tear ourselves away from the ennui of existence. Furthermore, *Littoral*, through its meaning, allowed Isabelle, Lucie Janvier and myself to define the vocation of the Théâtre Ô Parleur, anchoring it first and foremost in a theatre of language and ideas, a theatre that speaks out.

—Wajdi Mouawad

[1] The reference is to a passage in the 1868 novel *Les chants de Maldoror*, written by the Comte de Lautréamont, which describes dogs howling and running madly in all directions out of a thirst for the infinite.

Littoral (*Tideline*) was first produced at the Théâtre d'Aujourd'hui, Montreal, on June 2, 1997, during the 7th Theatre Festival of the Americas, with the following cast and crew:

Produced by Théâtre Ô Parleur
Directed by Wajdi Mouawad

Steve Laplante	Wilfrid
Gilles Renaud	Father
Claude Despins	Knight Guiromelan
Isabelle Leblanc	Simone
Pascal Contamine	Amé
David Boutin	Sabbé
Miro	Massi
Manon Brunelle	Josephine

Stage Manager and Production Director: Lucie Janvier
Set and Costumes by Charlotte Rouleau
Lighting by Michel Beaulieu
Original Music by Mathieu Farhoud-Dionne
Technical Director: Robert Lemoine

The first performance in France took place in Limoges, at the Théâtre de l'Union, on September 25, 1998 during the 15th Festival International des Francophonies de Limousin. Joel Bergeron took over the lighting for the production's first European tour, staying faithful to Michel Beaulieu's design.

CHARACTERS

Wilfrid
Father
Knight Guiromelan
Simone
Amé
Sabbé
Massi
Joséphine

There are many more speaking and non-speaking roles in the play. In the original production the additional speaking roles were distributed as follows:

Wilfrid
Father
Knight, Director, Servant, Farid, Moussa, Jamil
Simone, Script Supervisor, Girl in Bus Station, Aunt Marie, Housekeeper, Marie, Musician
Amé, Camera Person, Man in Bus Station, Uncle Emile, Henri, Doctor, Joseph, Guest
Sabbé, Boom Operator, Peep Show Customer, Sales Person, Uncle Michel, Young Father, Issam, Ghassane
Massi, Lighting Guy, Man 2 in Bus Station, Mortician, Agent, Uncle François, Adult Father, Old Woman, Ulrich, Hakim,
Josephine, Wardrobe Person, Girl in Bus Station, Clerk, Aunt Lucie, Jeanne, Script Supervisor (*scene 25*), Ankia, Madame Hakim

TRANSLATOR'S NOTE

The English translation incorporates cuts made by the author following the original French publication of *Littoral* by Leméac.

HERE

—— 1. Night ——

Night.

WILFRID

Sir, I ran all the way here to see you out of desperation. I was told you're the right person for this sort of thing, so I didn't hesitate, I came, even though they said you were very busy and never see anyone without an appointment, but people say all kinds of things. The proof: I'm here in front of you. That's a fact. I had to fight a bit with the bearded lady you have for a secretary, but it doesn't matter 'cause I'm here now in front of you. They also told me all I'd have to do is tell you my story. Tell you a bit about who I am. So I came as fast as I could to tell you who I am, but that's going to be kind of hard, because I'm young and these aren't the kind of things people talk about at my age. But what I *can* tell you is that my name is Wilfrid and I'm in a big hurry because of the laws of nature which very soon will start attacking from all sides. I can also tell you that this whole story started just three days ago and, if you want to know the truth, it started in an extraordinary way.

I was in bed with a goddess whose name I couldn't really remember. Annie or Julie or something, I don't really know, it's not that important, but it must have been something along those lines; and to tell you the whole truth, she didn't remember my name either and it suited both of us fine, Your Honour. We were going at it and it was amazing. I called her Lucy, Chantal, Annick, Marie and Siobhan; she called me William, Mustaffa, John, Federico and Claude; she also called me Gérard and Germain and it was amazing. We were inside each other, and that's how it went, exactly where we wanted it to.

Anyway, it was really great! That girl had an ass like you wouldn't believe, and I swear to you, Your Honour, I've had my hands on quite a few.

I don't want to go into too much detail because I can see it's neither the time or place, but it's important for me to tell you, important for you to know that right then, at that very moment, I was enjoying the best fuck of my life! A fuck, Your Honour, a real one, a good one, is a quick and easy injection of happiness and it's incredible. Your brain lights up and there's no bullshit about who loves who, there's just you living through your crotch, nothing else exists, and it's really great, and the thing to remember, Your Honour, in what I'm telling you, is that it was great! It was gluttonous, it was dirty, it was amazing. And when I came, it was in sync with the phone. It felt like I squirted three rings. Ejaculating a telephone is always quite a surprise, I'm not kidding. I won't say I shouldn't have answered, cause it's not true and anyway, it was still going to hit me in the face sooner or later. It's what you call fate. Some people don't believe in fate, I don't envy them, because anyway, I don't believe in it either. But this phone call at three in the morning, just when I was ejaculating, to tell me that my father had just died, if that wasn't destiny, what was it, for fuck's sake…?

I'm telling you right away that they called me at that ridiculous hour to inform me of my father's death just to spare you any emotional distress, since we're going to be together a good while and you'll have plenty of time to be moved. I don't want to bore the pants off you right off the bat. But when I answered the phone, I didn't know that my father just died and that *that* was why the phone was ringing, and that *that's* what I was about to find out. Hello? Yes, this is Wilfrid…. Yes…. Yes…. Yes…? Yes, that's him all right…. What do you mean am I sure…? What do you mean…? Huh…? What? What? What? What? Are you sure…? But how can it be…? No, I mean, what's he doing here…. What…? Yes…. Yes…. This can't be real – it's not true! No! No…! He's where…? He can't be – are you sure it's him? I'll be right there – what do you mean tomorrow morning…. You're closed…. How can you be closed? So why the hell did you call me? It's three in the morning and I was in the middle of screwing a girl with an ass to die for and you phone to give me one hell of a piece of news – shut up, you asshole, I'm talking – one hell of a piece of news and you tell me I can't come because you're closed? Why the hell did you call me then? What? What? So that I what? So I wouldn't worry? So I wouldn't worry – you called me so I wouldn't worry. I must be dreaming – tell me I'm dreaming. Listen, buddy, I don't know who you are and I couldn't care less, but I'm coming right over – I couldn't care less, you have no right, I've never heard anything like – exceptional circumstances my ass – and what's happening to me isn't an exceptional circumstance…? I don't care…. I don't give a shit, I want to see him…. I don't give a flying fuck about your gas leak – no, I won't stop yelling. Shit. What time do you open? Fine, I'll be there.

WILFRID hangs up.

I didn't stay home because I didn't want to be anywhere anymore. I went out to find a somewhere else, but it isn't easy when your heart is in your gut, which is a stupid expression. I looked everywhere for a somewhere else but I didn't find anything. Everywhere was still here, and it was exhausting.

—— 2. Film Shoot ——

Night. Outside. It's raining. WILFRID is walking. He's being followed by a film crew. DIRECTOR, CAMERA PERSON, BOOM OPERATOR, SCRIPT SUPERVISOR, LIGHTING PERSON, SOUND PERSON. They follow him as a group, shouldering a camera.

DIRECTOR
All right, we've only got half an hour for this scene! So let's get ready for a first take, and even if we do ten or twenty takes, make sure his makeup stays the same. It's a scene in the rain! *(to the LIGHTING DIRECTOR)* Take a light reading on his face, and remember we're shooting day for night. *(to the CAMERA PERSON)* I'll explain the first shot. Start from here. *(to the SCRIPT SUPERVISOR)* Give us a moment, please! (*to the CAMERA PERSON)* Pick him up here, we meet our protagonist, then you pull back a bit and that's when you start your long tracking shot that will bring you here to your final position, a wide shot, we see the utter solitude of the character. First positions everyone, we'll do a take.

SCRIPT SUPERVISOR
(throwing a bucket of water over WILFRID) We have continuity!

THE DIRECTOR
Start the rain machine!

BOOM OPERATOR
Sound rolling!

CAMERA PERSON
Camera rolling!

SCRIPT SUPERVISOR
Alone in the night, in the rain, take one.

DIRECTOR
Stand by! Three, two, one…! ACTION! Wilfrid. Keep walking. You're walking and you're thinking about your father's death, you're thinking about him, you're imagining that he probably died all alone, stabbed somewhere. You think about your father's face, his eyes, how helpless he felt dying all alone in some dark alleyway.

WILFRID
I don't know where I get this obsessive feeling that I'm always acting in a film.

DIRECTOR
Wilfrid, I don't exist, I know that very well, but do you know with absolute certainty whether you yourself exist? Is your life more real than mine? Walk, Wilfrid, walk. All of us here only exist in your gestures, your echoes, your comings and goings. Walk, Wilfrid, walk, walk…

WILFRID
I'm walking, I'm walking…

DIRECTOR
You're the only form that isn't boring, because you're always changing with our feelings, and you give us life.

WILFRID
I'm walking, I don't mind walking, but where to?

SCRIPT SUPERVISOR
Find a place where you can go get warm.

WILFRID
You're right, it is cold.

DIRECTOR
Wilfrid, we move through life like travellers who, struck by a sudden distraction, have lost track of where we're going. The film we're making is already so useless because we lack any memory and we've forgotten what we've filmed.

WILFRID
Shut up!

DIRECTOR
Okay, cut!

SCRIPT SUPERVISOR
Wilfrid, it's cold. And if you don't want to go back home, find a warm place you can stay until morning.

WILFRID
What do I need to get warm for? What's waiting for me in the morning? You're hilarious... you want me to spend the night getting warm so that in the morning I can go visit my father who's lying all alone in a fridge.

LIGHTING PERSON
But *we* don't want anything, Wilfrid, we're following you!

SCRIPT SUPERVISOR
We stay with you, Wilfrid, we're always with you.

CAMERA PERSON
Everywhere with you.

BOOM OPERATOR
Everywhere! Always everywhere.

LIGHTING PERSON
Always. Always. Endlessly.

DIRECTOR
I'm the director of this film, and I'm obsessed by a nameless anguish: Wilfrid, who are you? What strange world are you making us live in? Where are you dragging us? Into what cutthroat alley?

WILFRID
Shut up for fuck's sake, shut up, and get out of my head. Leave, go away! Leave me alone... I'm cold.

SCRIPT SUPERVISOR
What do you want, Wilfrid?

WILFRID
I want to see people, real people, not like you, I want to be with them, sit down with them, for the warmth of it.

BOOM OPERATOR
Go to the bus station. There are always people who go there for warmth.

WILFRID
Good idea. That way I'll see travellers, people arriving from somewhere else, people going somewhere else.

—— 3. Bus Station ——

Inside the bus station. A few people are asleep.

WILFRID
I don't want to talk about that too much cause it's not good for my image but you asked me to tell you everything. So I'm telling you. So that you'll be in a better position to judge afterwards, so that you can really judge my case in good conscience. But it's pressing, you understand, because the laws of nature are ruthless. According to the doctor, the corpse'll be okay for three days, maybe even four, but the doctor said that after four days he couldn't guarantee anything. So I rushed here to see you because they said I still had a chance, if you gave your authorization. Everywhere people told me you're the man to talk to, so I can tell you everything you want because you're the guy in charge, they said it's your job and you're the one who decides. But maybe not everything in my story will be true, and you mustn't hold it against me, because the truth of that night is stuck in my craw, I just want to shit it out, or vomit it out. Because at the bus station there was nothing. No warmth, no warmth, shit, no warmth, no warmth. There was a guy there with his drum and it filled me with hope, I don't know why. It must have been my grief. I don't know why. I saw my father down there in the morgue where I couldn't go identify him right away because of the gas leak, my father buck naked, in a refrigerator. A dead man in a freezer, that's hard to warm up, but that guy, with his big fat drum, he gave me such hope. I told myself something was going to happen.

A man is sleeping on a drum. He wakes up.

Do you smoke?

MAN
I got one left.

WILFRID
Can we share it?

MAN
I guess.

The man takes out his cigarette, lights it. They pass it back and forth.

WILFRID
My father's dead.

MAN
What do you mean, your father's dead?

WILFRID
I don't know. He died tonight. I was probably having sex when it happened. And some people say that's life. There's no life, dammit, there's nothing, nothing, you're stuck with an impossible mess that doesn't make any sense at all, not one iota, dammit. Is your father dead?

MAN
No, not yet.

WILFRID
How do you know.... He might be dying right now, stabbed in the back by someone who wants his money, or from a heart attack like what happens to old people when their heart gives out, maybe he committed suicide, who knows... maybe your father's dead and you don't know a thing, and his spirit is hanging around, right here, watching you sit there and have a smoke with me, completely unsuspecting, if, of course, what people say is true. But I don't believe it, I don't believe that afterwards the dead are always here or somewhere else, when they're dead; when they're dead, they're dead! Right. But oh my God, what if it *is* true? Life is such a bitch! You following me? Your father dies! And if it's true that there's something afterwards, it means that he can probably still see what's going on – that he's still everywhere,

always with you. Now in my case my father had only me in the whole world when he died, so if it's true what people say, then for sure the first thing he did was try to see me, to find out where I was, then he turns around and he sees his son in bed screwing his brains out, fucking some girl. He's dead, he turns around and he sees his son pumping away, hell, a girl screaming her head off and his ghost sees you shoot your spunk all over the place, everywhere, everywhere, everywhere, everywhere.... Shit, my father... I feel like I slept with—like I fucked—like I slept with death!

MAN
Where is he now?

WILFRID
In the morgue where I can't go, in the morgue, because they have a gas leak... a gas leak! I don't even know where the morgue is! Do you know where the morgue is?

MAN
Not really!

WILFRID
Shit.

MAN
Look in the phone book!

WILFRID
You wouldn't want to come with me? My name's Wilfrid. You?

MAN
Robert.

WILFRID
You wouldn't feel like coming with me to the morgue, Robert? I can't handle going all by myself!

MAN
Sure.

WILFRID
Am I ever lucky to have met you; there are so many pricks who don't even answer when you talk to them. But you're different, you're an artist, a musician, that's right, huh? You're a musician?

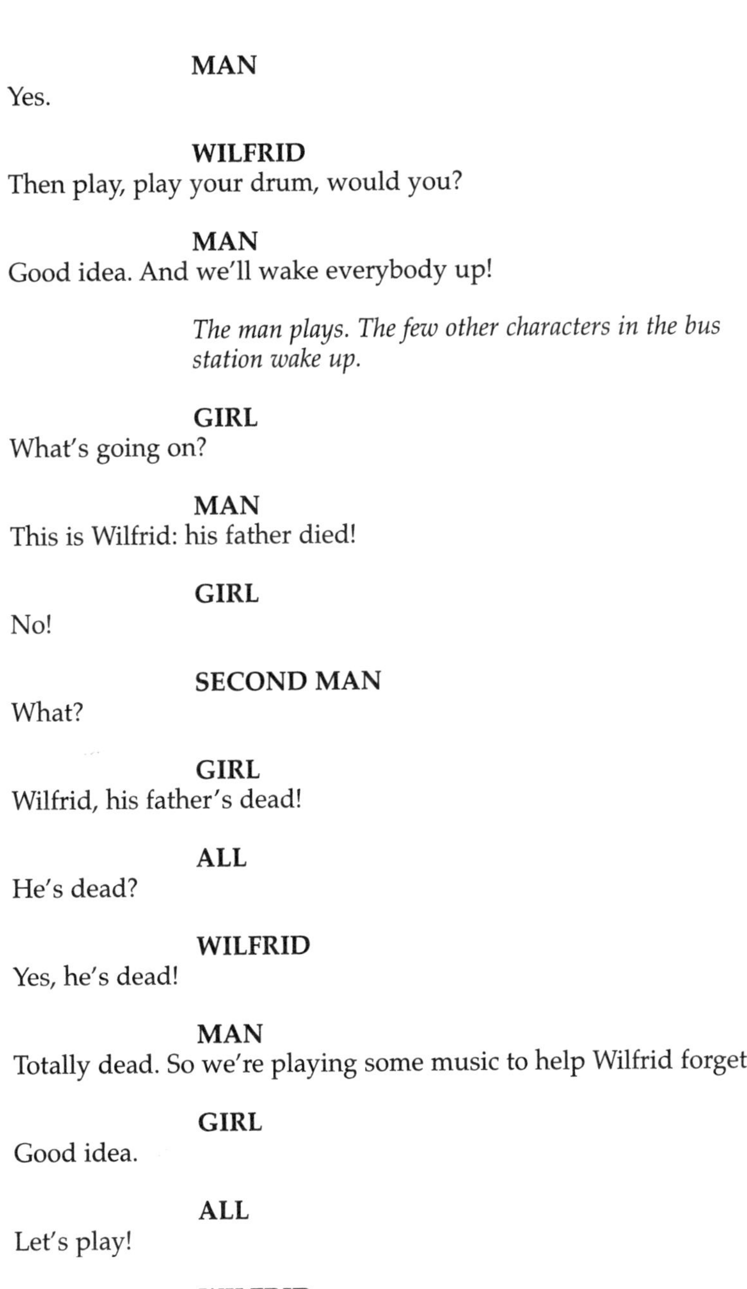

MAN
Yes.

WILFRID
Then play, play your drum, would you?

MAN
Good idea. And we'll wake everybody up!

The man plays. The few other characters in the bus station wake up.

GIRL
What's going on?

MAN
This is Wilfrid: his father died!

GIRL
No!

SECOND MAN
What?

GIRL
Wilfrid, his father's dead!

ALL
He's dead?

WILFRID
Yes, he's dead!

MAN
Totally dead. So we're playing some music to help Wilfrid forget.

GIRL
Good idea.

ALL
Let's play!

WILFRID
Yes, play, play, play!

SONG
Death Death Death is a blooming flower
To be plucked at its finest hour.

WILFRID
But nothing happened, nothing ever happened. His name probably wasn't even Robert. I don't know why I called him Robert. I don't know why I dreamed up that whole story. I don't know. I stayed in my head for a long, long, long long time, I summoned my film crew so they could go ahead with their routine shooting, then they left, somewhere, down there, to a far away country in my mind.... There's no soul, Your Honour, the soul doesn't exist, when you're dead, you're dead! And that's all, and I don't know why I'm here boring the shit out of you with my story, my "case" like the guy at the desk said. But I don't want to tell you just anything, I don't know why, I don't want to, I'm sure my father's in my head and I don't want him to find out I'm making up stories, because it's not true, I never went to the bus station that night. I never went into the bus station, the bus station was closed. I didn't want to go home, I was too afraid my father's ghost would be there. So I walked, and the only place open where I could go get warmed up was a Peep Show. When I got to the Peep Show, all the booths were taken, so I squeezed into the corner of a booth where there was already another guy.

—— 4. Peep Show ——

A Peep Show cubicle. Appropriate sound effects. WILFRID and the customer get acquainted.

CUSTOMER
Carl!

WILFRID
Wilfrid!

The chap immediately undoes his pants, the script supervisor and wardrobe person appear behind WILFRID, shouldering the camera.

CUSTOMER
(as soon as the film starts) Oh, shit.... Oh, the bitch! Ah, oh, shit, oh! She's sucking his cock.... Oh, shit, Oh! Her ass, did you see her

ass.... Oh, shit, look how he's taking her... oh yeah, oh yeah, oh yeah, oh yeah, go on, go on, go on, you bastard, oh yeah, keep going, oh, shit, oh, it's so... oh, I can't take it anymore, I can't take... I'm gonna come... shit that's good... that's good... look how hot she is, she's really something, Oh Yeah, you're something, you're really hot! Oh, your tits, your tits.... Oh, he's grabbing them, look at that... from behind, from behind! It's too much! I gotta stop, I gotta stop, I don't want to come yet – Oh, shit it's tough, it's really tough!

The film ends.

WILFRID
I have some change left if you want.

CUSTOMER
Not right away.... Shit do I ever love it! I love it!

WILFRID
You love what?

CUSTOMER
Peep Shows! I adore them...! I don't know, but I love jerking off in a booth, I love it, I don't know, I go at whatever rhythm I want, I'm doing myself. Shit, do I ever love it. There's no girl who takes me as far as I go here, all alone, in my own little booth.

CAMERA PERSON
Wilfrid, I just thought I'd mention, I don't mind shooting this but I don't think it's very healthy, and if I were you, I'd leave.

WILFRID
Nobody asked you to film this, buddy. Keep going.

WARDROBE PERSON
Wilfrid, this is wrong!

WILFRID
Let go of me!

CUSTOMER
Now I'm going to come, and then it'll be your turn, all right?

The film starts again.

Shit! Look at that, look at that, have you ever seen anything like it? Ah yes, you bitch! I'm slipping it into you, I'm sliding into you, I'm taking you, yes, I'm taking you, you bitch, goddammit, yeah, ah! Now, suck me, yes, yes, I'm going to come, I'm going to come, yes, suck it, keep sucking, harder, oh shit, it's good, it's so good, yes, Ah, Ah, Ah, Ah, Ah, Ah, AAAAaaaaaaaaAAAAAH!!!!

He comes in little bursts. Along with his last cry, we hear another cry approaching. Just when the CUSTOMER comes, suddenly a KNIGHT in armour appears, covered in blood, and finds himself standing face to face with WILFRID and the CUSTOMER as the CUSTOMER continues ejaculating.

KNIGHT
(at the sight of the customer ejaculating) AAAAaaaaaaAAAAAH!!!!

CUSTOMER
(at the sight of the bloody KNIGHT) AAAAaaaaaaAAAAAH!!!!

The KNIGHT slays the CUSTOMER with his sword.

KNIGHT
There, die, eyes omnivorous, heart perfidious. I've heard you in your filth, from the moment I began falling towards you, to meet you here and slit your throat, die black star, die! Ah! You stain, sullied flesh, a thousand times filth! Where am I? God! Even though I see myself awake, could I be dreaming? No, I'm not dreaming, I touch and I believe! And you, who are you, angel or devil? Speak before I strike you down!

WILFRID
My name is Wilfrid and my father is dead!

KNIGHT
Wilfrid is a name I understand. If your heart is as noble as your eyes, save me, for I am lost.

WILFRID
Who are you?

KNIGHT
I am the Knight Guiromelan. In the service of Arthur, my ailing king. I set off to search for the most Holy Grail, Morgan captured

me and carried me on her raven's wings screaming in my ears: "You, I won't kill. But I'll send you alive into hell." Someone make that moaning stop.

WILFRID
Not a possibility. You have to wait for it to stop by itself.

KNIGHT
Am I in hell then?!

WILFRID
If hell is a Peep Show, we're right in the flames.

KNIGHT
Get me out of here! For shame! Shame on those people and all that surrounds them. Shame, shame on evil, shame on filth, shame on waste! Wilfrid of the shining heart, deliver me from this nightmare, this nightmare where my hands, my feet, my heart and my mind are seized by the darkest torments. I no longer know who I am, what I'm doing or what I have to do! Help me, in the name of God who brought you here to rescue me, help me!

WILFRID
It's easy, take your sword and strike, smite everything, and say a prayer, and maybe that will launch you on your way and you'll take me with you, somewhere else, it doesn't matter where, but somewhere else, on your horse, far from here, far from death that's without meaning. Take your sword, Guiromelan, and decapitate everything in sight, go on, strike!

KNIGHT
I am a knight before God and I come from a world that doesn't know cowardice. Remove yourself from my path, naked images! On your knees, filth, on your knees!

WILFRID
We're taking off! We're taking off, knight, we're fleeing. Carry me on your wings, let's leave, I'm light, light, light, Guiromelan, keep going! Lift off, lift off, beat your wings!

KNIGHT
I'm beating, I'm beating!

WILFRID and the KNIGHT lift off. WILFRID finds himself beside the CUSTOMER.

CUSTOMER
Ah! That was good. Here, it's your turn.

WILFRID
No, that's fine! We're getting out of here!

SCRIPT SUPERVISOR, WARDROBE PERSON & CAMERA PERSON
Great idea!

WILFRID
Bye!

CUSTOMER
What do you mean, bye! Don't you want to have a little fun?

WILFRID
No thanks, I've had plenty of fun already.

—— 5. Dawn ——

WILFRID is walking down the street. It's dawn. Behind him we see the film crew following and filming surreptitiously.

WILFRID
Day was breaking, it was cold. I said to myself then that my father was dead, with the cold all around him, and those aren't the kind of thoughts that put you in a good mood, but I couldn't think about anything else. On the phone they told me they found him dead, sitting on a bench, not far from the pier where the boats come to dock. It's cold down there, and windy. Right at that moment I'd have liked to talk to him, ask him questions, but as hard as I concentrated, I couldn't make him come to me, even in my imagination he wouldn't come to me, I don't know why – in your mind you can make *anything* come to you, you just have to *want* to – *you* know very well, Your Honour, that you can do anything in your mind, since murderers have to be interrogated, hit on the head with phone books to make them confess what they're hiding in the recesses of their minds – but my father wouldn't

come, it's not like I didn't try to bang my head against a wall, I tried but it didn't do any good, my father wouldn't come, I concentrated as hard as I could, he still wouldn't come. I don't know. Maybe he thought my head was cluttered enough with all these shadows that follow me, that never give me any peace.

The crew has drawn closer to WILFRID.

Go away! I don't want to see you any more.

SCRIPT SUPERVISOR
What will you do without us, Wilfrid?

WILFRID
I'm not crazy, Your Honour, I'm simply telling you out loud what happens to everyone in whispers. In moments like this everyone talks to themselves at the risk of passing for a mental case. I don't want you to refuse my request, Your Honour. I think what I'm asking is very important. Yes, that's right, very important! For my father, but especially for me. I don't want to gloss over things too fast, Your Honour, and tell you just anything, but you'll find out that I wasn't born in the same country as my father. He was born over there, way over there, and I was born here. It was circumstances.... My father's dead, Your Honour. That night, when I left the Peep Show, I went over to the morgue. I don't know if you're like me, Your Honour, but I need proof to believe what people say. And I hadn't seen my father's body. Maybe it wasn't him who died, I said to myself, better make sure, you hear so many things about bums who steal wallets and then get murdered with other people's ID on them and it makes for a nasty surprise for the devastated family. I wasn't devastated because I wasn't sure yet what it meant to lose a father, but I can tell you, and you can believe me, when I got to the morgue I wasn't in great shape, because deep down I knew it couldn't be anyone else. I don't know if you're like me, Your Honour, but it was the first time I'd lost my father and I didn't know how to act. People tell you so little when you're young, so when things land on your head you're in deep shit.

—— 6. Morgue ——

WILFRID arrives at the morgue. Beside the corpse is a MORTICIAN.

WILFRID
So then I got to the morgue. The guy in the see-through coat, he's the one who cut up my father to find out what he died from. The man with the hat, that's my father.

MORTICIAN
Hello hello hello! Please excuse the smell, we had a gas leak. It's a bit early for this sort of thing, but before giving you the slightest detail, you have to identify the body. You're the son, correct?

WILFRID
Yes.

MORTICIAN
I'd have bet on it, there's quite a resemblance.

WILFRID
You knew my father?

MORTICIAN
I met him a little late. I'm the one who did the autopsy.

WILFRID
Oh! Pleased to meet you.

MORTICIAN
You really look like him. Come.

WILFRID
Are you sure it's necessary?

MORTICIAN
If you want to know what your father died of, you have to identify him first.

WILFRID
But since you say I look like him, he's as good as identified.

MORTICIAN
I don't have a choice. It's nothing, you'll see. It's never as bad as people imagine.

WILFRID
But I have a huge problem, you know, I imagine a lot…

MORTICIAN

Listen, don't get all worked up. It's only a corpse, the same kind of thing as the chicken carcass in your fridge. You'll see, it's no big deal, it's even a little green and it's really nothing, it's peaceful.

WILFRID

Peaceful, peaceful, you're hilarious! I know very well he's peaceful, *he's* not the problem, it's me!

MORTICIAN

Come on, come this way. It won't take long, I'll just uncover his face, just his face, that'll be enough.

WILFRID

I can't, I can't!

MORTICIAN

In that case, I can't give you your father's body.

WILFRID

But it's him, for fuck's sake!

MORTICIAN

It's him, but you still have to identify him! Here, look, it's not that hard, I'm looking at him, I see him, I'm staring at him and it isn't upsetting me at all!

WILFRID

I wouldn't brag if I were you! Of course it doesn't bother *you*, you spend your days up to your eyeballs in cadaver juice! For sure it won't upset *you*, but me – me – me knowing my father is there, knowing my father is there, naked, well, I can't handle it, that's all! Put yourself in my shoes! He's my father!

MORTICIAN

I embalmed my own, you know!

WILFRID

That's disgusting!

MORTICIAN

Of course, of course! My trade is repugnant, yet it's the most beautiful trade in the world!

WILFRID
To each his own.

MORTICIAN
When I leave here at the end of the day, I walk down the street and I look people in the eye and I laugh! Yes, I laugh, I laugh with happiness. Oh, a very simple happiness, very calm, very secret, a happiness all my own. Yes, I walk and I laugh looking into people's eyes because I see there what I never see in the eyes of my daily visitors here. A soul, a shining soul, the wonderful flame of life, the mysterious essence that gives each thing its meaning, I see it in the eyes of dogs, even pigeons. Walking down the street and looking into a child's eyes, that's the greatest happiness. Apart from that, it's quite pleasant here. It's just a matter of getting used to it. Come and see, your father isn't there anymore, his eyes are empty, his cheeks sunken, his soul absent.

WILFRID
Wait, I want to uncover him myself.

The MORTICIAN re-covers the corpse's face. WILFRID approaches it.

I know it's him, I know he's there, that it's his body. Never in my life have I felt lonely, because I've always been alone. But it feels like by lifting the sheet that separates me from this corpse I'm going to die too. Where are we? Where are we? And who am I, who am I? It's weird to go lift a sheet that's covering a corpse and then say: this is my father's corpse! It's bizarre. It's surreal. I know it's him. I don't need to lift up the sheet, I know it's him.

MORTICIAN
Then it's certain it's him.

WILFRID
Do you realize that nobody in the world except you knows I'm here?

MORTICIAN
Go on now. Lift the sheet.

WILFRID
It's him! It's him! My God, it's him! It's him, it's his face, his face, it's his face, my father's face, my father, it's him.... Is it ever awful here, it's macabre!

MORTICIAN
I'll walk you to the door, you've been here too long.

WILFRID
I want to be alone with him for a moment, just a moment!

MORTICIAN
I'm not allowed to leave you alone!

WILFRID
But you can trust me, don't worry, I won't eat the corpse, I just want to be alone with him for a moment.

MORTICIAN
I'm sorry, I can't allow it!

WILFRID
I want to see him again.

MORTICIAN
I'm not sure that's a good idea.

WILFRID
Go to hell, I want to see him one last time. I'd really like to be all alone with him.

MORTICIAN
It isn't possible!

WILFRID
No one's going to stop me from being alone with my father's corpse!

MORTICIAN
I'm going to ask you to leave immediately.

WILFRID
Never.

MORTICIAN
I won't repeat myself, if you don't leave immediately, I'll have you forcibly removed!

WILFRID
No force will be able to remove me from here. Because I have a secret weapon: an invincible friend!

MORTICIAN
That I'd like to see!

WILFRID
Well, you just have to ask! GUIROMELAN!!!

The KNIGHT in armour appears before MORTICIAN.

KNIGHT
AAAAAAaaaaaaaaaaAAAAAAAAAAH!!!!

MORTICIAN
AAAAAAaaaaaaaaaaAAAAAAAAAAH!!!!

The MORTICIAN crumples and writhes in a horrible cardiac convulsion.

KNIGHT
I came running as soon as I heard your call.

WILFRID
My father died, Guiromelan.

KNIGHT
That's something every good father should do before his son.

WILFRID
My heart is emptying, Guiromelan, like a punctured pail. Who is my father? Who is this corpse that was my father? Is your father dead, Guiromelan?

KNIGHT
My king is ailing. A dark melancholy has overtaken him, he doesn't respond anymore, his heart is heavy. He is despairing.

WILFRID
What are we going to do?

KNIGHT
Dream.

WILFRID
It hurts to dream all the time. It makes you crazy, but the most painful thing about the dream is that it doesn't exist.

KNIGHT
What are you talking about? What about me, what am I? What am I? Nothing? I don't exist? Now what? I am the Knight Guiromelan, who set off in search of the Holy Grail and was precipitated here, into this strange world, by Morgan.

WILFRID
You don't exist, Guiromelan, you don't exist. You aren't good for anything, because you only exist in my head.

KNIGHT
What are you talking about! Dreams are at the heart of life. We dream our lives, and we live our dreams. Look at me. I am your dream, you are my life. I am the flame that blazes deep inside you. You are the eyes through which I burn. Stand up. A Knight stands tall, he doesn't even look at the horizon, he directs his gaze even further to the north, to the south, to the east and to the west.

WILFRID
Carry me away on the wings of your dragon, Guiromelan. I've had enough. Carry me away, I can't take it anymore! I just want to die and be at peace! A morgue is a wonderful place to die! You let yourself go and they look after you with the most insane pleasure. Take your sword and finish me off, let's get it over with! I'm sick of everything.

KNIGHT
All right. I'm going to kill you.

WILFRID
No, wait wait wait… wait a bit!

KNIGHT
Fear not, Wilfrid, a dream can't kill. It makes things different, but it doesn't kill. I'll prove it:

The KNIGHT kills WILFRID. WILFRID crumples. The MORTICIAN revives WILFRID.

MORTICIAN
I knew you shouldn't have looked twice.

WILFRID
I passed out!

KNIGHT
For a moment! Yes, you fainted.

MORTICIAN
Come, I'll escort you to the door. When you leave, we'll give you an envelope in which you'll find the results of the autopsy. I've spared you the photographs.

WILFRID
What's going to happen with my father's body?

KNIGHT
Somewhere down there exists a magnificent place full of light to welcome your father's body.

MORTICIAN
That depends on your means.

KNIGHT
A still unknown place, that exists only to welcome your father's body.

MORTICIAN
If you want him cremated without a viewing, it isn't very expensive, quite economical in fact, but otherwise you can have a viewing, then either bury him or cremate him, with or without a service, with or without flowers, with a small car or a big car, two big cars, three big cars, it depends on your means, your beliefs. You simply have to go to the second floor, ask for information, choose the arrangements that suit you and we take care of everything.

WILFRID
I don't feel very well.

KNIGHT
What are you doing with your father's body? Into whose hands are you abandoning him?

WILFRID
Let go of me!

MORTICIAN
Actually, when your father was found he had a bit of money on him, his identification, and a red suitcase the police held on to. To collect everything, just go to the police station, which is up on the third floor.

WILFRID
I'm sorry sir but I have to leave.

MORTICIAN
Come, I'll see you to the door.

WILFRID
Thank you, but I'll go by myself. It's not that I don't like you, but actually, I don't.

—— 7. Promise ——

WILFRID and the KNIGHT are walking. It's daytime.

WILFRID
I'm sorry about what happened at the morgue. I didn't mean to be an idiot.

KNIGHT
That's all right. I didn't take it personally. You're going through a difficult time.

WILFRID
You came at an awkward moment.

KNIGHT
You're the one who summons me!

WILFRID
So when I tell you to leave, leave!

KNIGHT
I'm sorry but when somebody summons me, they summon me, I don't make round trips. When I arrive, I stay. Deal with it.

I might not be convenient, but on the other hand, I've never let you down, right?

WILFRID
That's true…!

KNIGHT
When you were little, how many times did I come and save you?

WILFRID
Often, every night, you always came to save the day.

KNIGHT
Back then I was an astronaut crossing light years to land in your closet. Then you kept me hidden in your room and I taught you the secrets of the universe.

WILFRID
You were an astronaut for a long time. Now you're a Knight, sometimes you become the filmmaker. I really put you through a lot.

KNIGHT
I'd be nothing without you!

WILFRID
Don't say that…

KNIGHT
If only you knew! I really would have liked to exist too. I'd have liked to feel, I'd have liked to dream, be upset, be sad, be happy, but what can you do? I don't exist and sometimes that's a bit hard to live with. I wander in your mind, depending on you to feel. Being upset because you're upset, being happy because you're happy.

WILFRID
Don't worry about it. Feeling isn't all that much fun, because in general, life always makes you feel the same thing. It tests you in one direction, then it won't let you go and everything you experience always has the same flavour. My father is dead. You think that upsets me? I'm not upset, I'm a little surprised, astonished, but I'm not sad.

KNIGHT
I saw you crying at the morgue, while you were looking at your father's body.

WILFRID
When I saw the corpse, I felt like I was looking at a suit that had no more purpose. My father left without feeling the need to take his one and only real garment. So that made me cry. The guy showed me the suit and I had to say with the utmost seriousness: Yes, yes, that's what my father used to wear. A pie in the face like that, that's a good reason to cry.

KNIGHT
When you were little and would get up in the middle of the night for a glass of water, we would fight the monsters hiding in the hallway. A monster is big and ugly, it's easy to fight, and we were always the victors. Now I'm a weary knight who doesn't know what he's supposed to wield his sword against. You've grown up, Wilfrid, and the monsters have become much too powerful. My sword isn't enough to comfort you.

WILFRID
I don't even know who I am anymore so how can I know what's hurting me? When you're little, it's easy, all kids are scared of the same thing. Of the big bad wolf or monsters from outer space. But now? Why do I hurt? I really don't have a clue. I hurt and that's it. And everyone's hurting and nobody gives a damn! What do you want me to tell you? No, your sword is useless against all that! My mother died bringing me into the world, my father died while I was screwing like a madman so now I'm all alone and I'm a little pissed off at myself, you understand? I'm a little pissed off at myself for having killed my mother and for having slept with my father because, yes, when you have sex, you're doing it with all those who die at the moment you spill yourself deep into somebody, and I spilled myself deep into my father just like I spilled my mother's blood, leaving her there, lying there in her bed. Guiromelan, I'm telling you, I don't know by what miracle I have enough imagination left to believe in you, but today, if I abandon you or if you abandon me, there'll be a gaping hole deep inside me that I'll fall into and disappear.

KNIGHT
I'll never abandon you. Without you, I'm nothing, you dream about me and I exist.

WILFRID
And as for me, I'll never forget *you.*

KNIGHT
How could you forget me? By forgetting me you'd kill me. And I'd a thousand times rather you kill me than leave me behind on the shore of your memory. Wilfrid, I'll make you a knight's promise: Despite our hearts' disasters, we will ever be true to each other. My friendship for you is so deep that in spite of you I will remain your strength. Your friendship is so bright that you need only say the word and I, poor dream that I am, will set off towards you. Wilfrid, nothing is stronger than the dream that binds us forever.

—— 8. Procedures ——

WILFRID is in two offices and a store. A CLERK and a funeral AGENT, a SALESPERSON.

CLERK
Sir?

AGENT
Hello, sir.

SALESPERSON
Can I help you sir?

WILFRID
I was told to come and see you. I was sent to come and see you. I need to see you.

CLERK
What is it regarding?

AGENT
Regarding what?

WILFRID
It's for my father's effects. My father's effects. My father.

SALESPERSON
Is it for a suit or a jacket?

AGENT
Do you need a flower arrangement?

WILFRID
Yes, ma'am, a suit, and it's urgent.

SALESPERSON
Is it for a wedding?

CLERK
What is it for?

WILFRID
No, sir, for a funeral.

AGENT
He can be viewed as of tomorrow.

WILFRID
I was told there was a red suitcase and a small amount of money.

CLERK
I need some proof of identity.

AGENT
Or, if you don't want a viewing…

WILFRID
Here, sir.

SALESPERSON
What size do you take?

AGENT
…he can, still, as of tomorrow, either be cremated or buried.

CLERK
I'll be right back.

WILFRID
I have no idea, sir!

SALESPERSON
I'll take care of everything!

WILFRID
Yes, as of tomorrow, that would be fine.

AGENT
What would you like?

WILFRID
To have a viewing, madam.

SALESPERSON
Raise your arms.

AGENT
Where would you like to have him buried?

WILFRID
It was at that moment, Your Honour, precisely then, that I was suddenly overcome with anguish. I didn't have any idea where I should bury my father, I wasn't at all familiar with the process of finding a place to bury someone. The woman said to me:

AGENT
Don't worry, sir.

SALESPERSON
Don't worry, sir.

AGENT
If you like, we can take care of everything…

SALESPERSON
I'll take care of everything.

AGENT
…and find you a place according to your beliefs and your means.

WILFRID
It was all well and good, and also very kind…

SALESPERSON
This suit is a perfect fit!

WILFRID
…but there was my mother, my mother, Your Honour. My mother died here, since I was born here, and my mother died bringing

me into the world, I think I've already told you that. Anyway, Your Honour, it seemed to me that the right thing would be for my father to be buried with my mother, since he'd been madly in love with her and went mad when she died. But I sensed that would be very complicated because of my mother's family who are very rich and who have a family crypt and who are very stingy about the space in said crypt. I'd have liked to have done this in private, Your Honour, but if I wanted my father to be in the arms of my mother forever, I'd have to put on a good show and have a viewing, and then I'd have a chance that the family would agree. I have to tell you, Your Honour, that my father wasn't very well liked.

CLERK

Here's the suitcase. And here are the personal effects your father had with him.

SALESPERSON

I won't charge you the tax, you're miserable enough as it is.

WILFRID

Thank you sir. I had to notify the family. And, Your Honour, I really didn't feel up to it. The mere idea of phoning to tell them the news made me queasy. Because those people, Your Honour, I don't want to say anything bad about them, but they're something else. My father's suitcase under my arm, I went back to my apartment and I phoned from there. My first Aunt could barely restrain herself from jumping for joy. And then she started phoning everyone and everybody came.

—— 9. The Family ——

WILFRID's home. WILFRID's aunts and uncles rush over to him.

AUNT MARIE

Wilfrid!

UNCLE MICHEL

My God! Wilfrid!

AUNT LUCIE

What a tragedy!

AUNT MARIE
It's dreadful!

ALL
Horrible!

AUNT MARIE
Truly horrible!

UNCLE FRANÇOIS
Oh yes!

AUNT MARIE
Aaaaaaayyyyy!

UNCLE MICHEL
Marie! Really, you're not going to start to cry, are you!

AUNT LUCIE
What will you do now, Wilfrid?

UNCLE FRANÇOIS
What are you going to do?

UNCLE MICHEL
Yes, what *are* you going to do?

UNCLE ÉMILE
He's not going to do anything! What do you expect him to do?

AUNT LUCIE
Émile! Please! Try to be a bit gentler with the boy!

UNCLE ÉMILE
What? You're all asking him what he's going to do. But in situations like this, there's nothing to do except keep your mouth shut!

AUNT MARIE
Émile! Please! You're talking to your dead sister's son! Have a bit of respect!

UNCLE ÉMILE
What do you mean, a bit of respect? I'm showing all my respect to my sister's son. How am I not showing respect to my sister's son, can you tell me?

AUNT LUCIE
His father is dead!

AUNT MARIE
Aaaaaaaayyyyyy!

UNCLE MICHEL
Please, Marie, you're not going to start crying!

UNCLE ÉMILE
I know he's dead! So, he's dead! What can you do about it? There's nothing to be done! The boy went to the morgue, he identified the body, and that's where it ends! We're going to help him bury him, and that's all! I mean, we're not going to get our balls in a knot just because the guy croaked! He's dead, he's dead!

KNIGHT
AAAAAAaaaaaaaaaaAAAAAAAAAH!!!!

WILFRID
No! Film it instead, it'll be a lot more interesting!

UNCLE FRANÇOIS
Wilfrid, what do you want us to do? Look at us, we're your family.

AUNT MARIE
Your mother was our eldest sister.

AUNT LUCIE
She raised us even, all three of us.

UNCLE FRANÇOIS
Yes, she brought them up, your Aunt Marie, your Aunt Lucie, your Uncle Émile, so you understand, we're with you and we want to help you. Whether it's moral support or financial help, you can count on us!

AUNT LUCIE
Absolutely! Wilfrid!

AUNT MARIE
My God! Poor child! Aaaaaayyyy!

UNCLE MICHEL
Please, Marie, you're not going to cry!

AUNT MARIE
Ahhhh!

AUNT LUCIE
Aaaaaayyyy!

UNCLE FRANÇOIS
You're not going to start too!

AUNTS MARIE & LUCIE
Aaaaaaaayyyy! Aaaaaahhhh!! Aaaaaaaayyyy!

UNCLE FRANÇOIS
Is there anything we can do for you, Wilfrid?

WILFRID
Yes.

UNCLE MICHEL
Oh really?

ALL
What?

WILFRID
I'd like my father to be buried with my mother.

UNCLE ÉMILE
Well!

AUNT MARIE
Émile, don't get worked up, please!

AUNT LUCIE
My God!

UNCLE ÉMILE
I knew it would come to this, I knew it!

AUNT MARIE
Émile, please, don't get worked up!

UNCLE ÉMILE
I'm not getting worked up! But did you hear what he just said, this is unbelievable, it's scandalous, the gall!

AUNT LUCIE
Émile, don't get all upset!

AUNT MARIE
Don't get all upset, Émile!

UNCLE ÉMILE
Stop telling me not to get upset, it's upsetting me!

AUNTS MARIE & LUCIE
Aaaaaaaaaaaayyyy!

UNCLE MICHEL
Marie, you aren't going to start crying now!

WILFRID
Listen! I know you didn't like my father very much, but if you really want to do something for me, you could understand that my parents loved each other very much and deserve to be together again after 26 years apart.

UNCLE ÉMILE
You must be joking, tell me I'm dreaming!

AUNT MARIE
But we liked your father a lot, why do you say we didn't like him?

AUNT LUCIE
We liked him a lot!

UNCLE FRANÇOIS
That's a good one!

WILFRID
Listen, it doesn't matter whether you liked him or not, anyway, he felt the same way about you. That's not the issue.

AUNT MARIE
So?

AUNT LUCIE sobs deeply.

WILFRID
The issue is that two people loved each other and now they're both dead. I don't know, but put yourself in my shoes…

AUNT MARIE
But we're trying!

AUNT LUCIE
Yes, we're trying!

AUNT MARIE
That's all we're doing!

UNCLE FRANÇOIS
Like hell!

UNCLE ÉMILE
Except we don't understand!

WILFRID
It seems pretty simple to me! Everyone here is going to be buried with their spouse, right…? You all already have your places reserved, right?

UNCLE FRANÇOIS
Yes.

UNCLE ÉMILE
So?!

WILFRID
So why shouldn't my father have the right to be buried with my mother? Or, if you prefer, if you really want to bring it closer to home, why shouldn't my mother, your sister, have the right to be buried with my father, her husband? It seems to me that goes without saying, doesn't it? It seems to me that would be a way to thank her, my mother, the sister who brought you up so well. I don't get it! You've told me so many things about my mother, for Christ's sake! Every time I come to visit, you talk about my mother! You've told me a thousand times that she's the one who raised you when your parents died and you were still only children! And she's the one who helped you get married, you, Aunt

Marie to Uncle Michel, and you Aunt Lucie to Uncle François, and you Uncle Émile, how many times did you tell me that without my mother you'd still be rotting in a prison back in your country! How many times did you tell me that without my mother you were nothing? How many times did all of you tell me how my mother helped you escape your country with your children when the war came, how she helped you come and settle here, how many times did you tell me things about my mother, that she waited for all of you to be married before getting married herself – how many times for fuck's sake? So it seems to me that it would make sense for you to do her this favour, to let the man she loved lie beside her for all eternity!

AUNT MARIE

When your mother died, Wilfrid, we gave her the most beautiful place in the family crypt.

AUNT LUCIE

We owed it to her!

WILFRID

I don't care if it's the most beautiful place in the crypt. It may be the most beautiful place, but it's still a cold and lonely place!

AUNT MARIE

Don't be mean, Wilfrid; we loved your mother very much…

AUNT LUCIE

Only…

WILFRID

Only what?

AUNT MARIE

Only… that!

AUNT LUCIE

Your father…

WILFRID

What, my father…?

UNCLE ÉMILE

Uh, well, your father was the worst kind of bastard, there it is!

UNCLE FRANÇOIS
Come on! Émile–

UNCLE ÉMILE
And as long as I live, that man will never be buried with our sister. I don't know why we're arguing, because we can argue about it for ten thousand years, it won't change a thing, that man will never be buried in the family crypt. There. And what I find scandalous and what doesn't surprise me either about that man, is that he didn't let you know!

AUNT MARIE
Émile, the boy, really!

UNCLE ÉMILE
Well, the boy is a man now and it's high time he had an idea what happened, so he'll understand! It's outrageous – the nerve that with the miserable debauched life he led, he never told his son that it was understood between us for a long time that never with a capital "N" would he be buried with his wife in his wife's family crypt.

AUNT LUCIE
Émile!

UNCLE ÉMILE
Well, it was understood!

UNCLE FRANÇOIS
Yes, yes, it was understood.

UNCLE ÉMILE
We had an understanding!

UNCLE FRANÇOIS
Yes, yes!

UNCLE ÉMILE
So why didn't that bastard make his own arrangements before he croaked? Why didn't he find a place so he wouldn't bug our asses from the graves!

AUNT LUCIE
Émile, Émile!

UNCLE ÉMILE

What, Émile, Émile, for Christ's sake! We have to explain it to him properly, don't we? He's here yelling at us about his mother! He didn't know his mother – did he know his mother? He didn't know her! Did you know her?

WILFRID

No but–

UNCLE ÉMILE

So what are you doing being a pain in the ass with stories about how your mother was madly in love with your father. Her only madness was following that man, but she never loved him, how can she have loved him, he was never there, always gallivanting around, always everywhere except with her!

UNCLE FRANÇOIS

That's enough, Émile!

UNCLE ÉMILE

You, shut up!

KNIGHT

Are you sure you don't want me to shut him up?

WILFRID

Forget it!

UNCLE ÉMILE

And him, he never loved her, he used her, he exploited her, right up to the end, to the very end!

AUNT LUCIE

Émile, I'm begging you–

UNCLE ÉMILE

To the very end, yes! And you know what I'm thinking about when I say to the end! That bastard! And then this little jerk comes and lectures us about what we should do to thank that woman! But *you* didn't know her, so shut your mouth! He sounds like his father – just like his father! He didn't even bother to teach you the accent of our homeland! You talk like a foreigner, with a foreign accent to the members of your family!

WILFRID
I didn't know you hated him that much. What did he do to you? What happened to make you call him a bastard even on the day he dies? What's this all about?

AUNT MARIE
Listen, Wilfrid, your Uncle Émile loved your mother very much and when she died, he was beside himself with grief.

WILFRID
What does that have to do with my father?!

AUNT MARIE
Wilfrid. We loved your father, only he was a little different and he made certain mistakes that caused a certain tension between us, but that wasn't the problem.

WILFRID
I have no idea what you're talking about!

AUNT MARIE
The fact is that there's no room in the crypt for your father, all the places are already reserved. But if you want, we can find a little place in the cemetery, not too far away.

AUNT LUCIE
That's a good idea!

WILFRID
I don't know.

UNCLE ÉMILE
In any case, forget about the crypt.

WILFRID
Listen. As of tomorrow morning, my father will be on view in the funeral home for the next three days. The mortician told me I could wait until the third day to tell them where he'll be buried. So don't give me an answer right away, think it over seriously, and then we'll talk about it again.

UNCLE ÉMILE
You don't understand that it's already been thought through completely! No! The answer's no!

UNCLE FRANÇOIS
Wilfrid's right. We can take some time to think it over.

AUNT MARIE
Very well. That's a good idea.

UNCLE ÉMILE
What do you mean that's a good idea?

AUNT MARIE
Émile! I said it was a good idea.

UNCLE ÉMILE
But what good is a good idea when in any case we're going to tell him "no." Whether we say so now or in three days, it's no!

AUNT MARIE
Émile, please! The boy has a lot on his mind! Tomorrow is his first day in the funeral home, and we didn't come to his little apartment tonight to upset him!

AUNT LUCIE
Are you happy with the funeral home at least?

WILFRID
It's all right. It's a funeral home. You can see him there, it's nothing fancy.

UNCLE MICHEL
But it's very nice for a funeral home!

UNCLE ÉMILE
I say it's time he knew who his father really was.

UNCLE MICHEL
It's really very nice for a funeral home.

UNCLE FRANÇOIS
Very good. It's bright and cozy at the same time.

UNCLE ÉMILE
He should know once and for all.

AUNT LUCIE
The body isn't here yet?

WILFRID
They're preparing it.

UNCLE ÉMILE
I'm not afraid to tell him, I'm not afraid to speak the truth out loud! Wait – where are you now?

AUNT MARIE
What do you mean where are we?

UNCLE ÉMILE
Yes, where are you now?

AUNT LUCIE
We're at the funeral home!

UNCLE ÉMILE
Since when are we at the funeral home?

AUNT LUCIE
Since a few moments ago, I mean–

UNCLE ÉMILE
Listen! Maybe *you're* at the funeral home, but *I'm* not.

UNCLE FRANÇOIS
So where are *you*?

UNCLE ÉMILE
I'm still at Wilfrid's apartment.

UNCLE MICHEL
What are you doing there?

UNCLE ÉMILE
I was talking quietly in the kitchen, and you suddenly tell me that we're at the funeral home! But I haven't finished, I still have things to get off my chest, goddammit! I'm in Wilfrid's apartment and you're going to stay here with me until I've finished.

UNCLE FRANÇOIS
Stop being a pain in the ass and just accept like everyone else that now we're at the funeral home!

UNCLE ÉMILE
Out of the question. We're in Wilfrid's apartment!

AUNT MARIE
Come on, Émile, be reasonable, you see very well that everyone agrees we're at the funeral home, so stop it.

UNCLE ÉMILE
But I haven't finished talking!

AUNT MARIE
Well then, you'll finish talking at the funeral home and that'll be that! The story's complicated enough as it is.

AUNT LUCIE
You're absolutely right!

UNCLE ÉMILE
But you won't let me talk at the funeral home. You're going to tell me it's not a place for talking and you'll manage to shut me up again!

AUNT MARIE
Don't be silly, we won't stop you from talking!

UNCLE FRANÇOIS
How could you think that!

AUNT LUCIE
Honestly!

WILFRID
So what are we doing? Where are we now? In my apartment or at the funeral home?

UNCLE ÉMILE
You are such pains in the ass!

AUNT MARIE
Come on, Émile, say it so we can move things along a little.

UNCLE ÉMILE
But you won't stop me from talking?

AUNT LUCIE
Of course not!

UNCLE ÉMILE
Then all right, we're in the funeral home!

ALL
Aha!

UNCLE MICHEL
Just in time!

—— 10. Funeral Home ——

At the funeral home. The FATHER's body is there. The AUNTS sob and wail.

AUNT MARIE
Aaaaaaaaaaayyyy!!

UNCLE FRANÇOIS
My condolences.

WILFRID
Thank you.

AUNT LUCIE
Aaaaahhh!!!

UNCLE MICHEL
My condolences.

WILFRID
Thank you.

AUNT MARIE
Aaaaaahhh!!

AUNT LUCIE
Oooooh!

UNCLE ÉMILE
My condolences.

WILFRID
Thank you.

AUNT MARIE
Wilfrid, bunny, my poor little Wilfrid. What will become of you?

AUNT LUCIE
Aaaaaaaayyyy!

UNCLE ÉMILE
Maybe he could have him cremated.

UNCLE MICHEL
That would be a solution.

UNCLE ÉMILE
That would solve the whole problem.

UNCLE FRANÇOIS
I'll say.

AUNT LUCIE
Aaaaaaaaaayyyy!

UNCLE ÉMILE
That'll take care of it. Less complicated, less cumbersome and less costly.

UNCLE FRANÇOIS
That's not the issue. If it's a question of money, we're here to help the boy.

AUNT MARIE
Oooooh!

AUNT LUCIE
Eeeeeaaah!

UNCLE ÉMILE
Well I'm not giving him a cent!

UNCLE MICHEL
Then people will say you're a tightwad.

AUNT MARIE
Eeyaah!

UNCLE ÉMILE
I couldn't care less what people say!

AUNT LUCIE
Ayyyyyyy!

UNCLE FRANÇOIS
That's easy to say!

UNCLE ÉMILE
Yes, it's easy to say! And that's what I say. Yes. I'm not afraid to say what I think.

UNCLE FRANÇOIS
Don't we know it!

UNCLE ÉMILE
And believe you me, I don't give a damn what people think.

AUNT MARIE
Ayyyyyyy!

AUNT LUCIE
My God.

UNCLE ÉMILE
I'm not giving a cent to bury that sonovabitch.

UNCLE FRANÇOIS
Shut your trap!

UNCLE ÉMILE
What do you mean shut my trap? Since when do I have to shut my trap! Bugger off with your "shut your traps!"

AUNT MARIE
Will the two of you cut that out!?

AUNT LUCIE

Honestly!

UNCLE ÉMILE

Obviously it's not *your* sister who's dead.

UNCLE FRANÇOIS

I said take your hands off me!

UNCLE ÉMILE

You're starting to get up my ass! Let's have it out.

AUNT MARIE

Émile!

AUNT LUCIE

François! For heaven's sake, let go of each other, let go of each other!

WILFRID

Will you stop, already, will you calm down, I've had enough of you pissing me off!

AUNT MARIE

My God! Thank God no one was here to see us! I'm so embarrassed, I'm absolutely mortified.

WILFRID

All right, quit yelling and tell me what happened! Why didn't you like my father?

UNCLE ÉMILE

If you want to know the whole story, my boy, have a seat and hold on to your shorts 'cause it's gonna blow your head off!

AUNT MARIE

Émile, I don't think it's a good idea!

UNCLE ÉMILE

It's time you knew, Wilfrid, that your father killed your mother.

AUNT LUCIE

My God, Émile. Stop it!

AUNT MARIE
Don't listen to him, Wilfrid, it isn't true, it isn't true!

UNCLE ÉMILE
Your mother was much too fragile to have a child, she knew that, the doctors had told her, she was too fragile, the doctors repeated it a thousand times! And when she got pregnant he forced her to keep the child, he forced her, we all encouraged your mother to have an abortion, to forget about it, but not him, the child was more important, so he forced her to keep it, that damned foetus, and when the child was born, obviously, she wasn't strong enough and she died!

WILFRID
What child are you talking about!?

UNCLE ÉMILE
You! What other child could it be!

Silence.

FATHER
Pssst! Wilfrid… Wilfrid…. Pssst!

WILFRID
Dad!

FATHER
Shhhhh!

WILFRID
What on earth – I must be dreaming!

FATHER
Let's get out of here!

WILFRID
What do you mean, let's get out of here?

FATHER
We'll wait till they have their backs turned, and we'll make a run for it!

WILFRID
But you're dead!

FATHER
You make everything sound worse than it is.

WILFRID
So you aren't dead?

FATHER
What difference does it make?

WILFRID
Uh… no difference… except that–

KNIGHT
Their backs are turned…

FATHER
Quick! Let's go! We'll explain ourselves later!

WILFRID
Dad! Dad! Wait for me! Wait for me!

FATHER
Run!

KNIGHT
Run, Wilfrid, go, fly, follow that unbeaten path that leads to the abyss, and jump! Jump into the abyss! Forget the roads, because all roads lead to the earth, the abyss only leads to the dream. Jump, Wilfrid, jump!

YESTERDAY

In this section we see the father at three different ages. The YOUNG FATHER represents the time when the mother JEANNE was alive. The ADULT FATHER represents the time after the mother's death. The FATHER is the dead father.

—— 11. Ghost ——

WILFRID arrives home. It's evening.

WILFRID

The worst thing in this sort of situation, Your Honour, I mean, when you have no one left in the world, is that you wonder how the next morning you'll find enough strength to keep on doing what you were doing the night before. I don't know if you understand me, Your Honour, but last night, when I got home after that wonderful first day at the funeral home, I honestly started to resent my father for getting me into this situation. It was no picnic, let me tell you, and I still hadn't slept for two days, Your Honour, but as much as I tossed and turned in my bed, I couldn't manage to catch even a couple of winks. Even masturbating, Your Honour, hasn't provided any comfort or distraction. So it's real despair. But when you don't have a choice, there's only one solution left. So the dreams surface in the night, in my mind, Guiromelan is a prisoner in an era the shape of a dungeon. He fights, but how can you fight a wall, I'm a famous actor and I'm acting in a film, it's a film about a young man with no idea where to bury his father…. He's one of the most talented actors to come along in the last 20 years, people just can't get over how talented he is… Guiromelan… is a prisoner, he doesn't know how to escape… his King is dying…

Enter the FATHER.

FATHER

Wilfrid, I'm cold. I'm cold. I'm afraid and I'm cold. My blood is petrified, my breath frozen. Wilfrid, light doesn't touch me anymore. This morning I was astonished to see it so far from me, never reaching me, always far away, diffused. Wilfrid!

WILFRID wakes up with a cry.

WILFRID

Dad!

FATHER

Good evening, Wilfrid.

WILFRID

Dad!

FATHER

Did you just have a bad dream?

WILFRID

I dreamt you were dead.

FATHER

Well, you see? I'm fine.

WILFRID

And you've come to see me?

FATHER

We haven't seen each other for quite a while.

WILFRID

And you're not dead?

FATHER

I'm not dead.

WILFRID

I'm so happy to see you!

WILFRID wakes up, he's alone.

I'm losing my mind, I'm losing it, losing it, losing it...
So then, Your Honour, I picked up the suitcase and I opened it.

FATHER

Wilfrid.

WILFRID

Dad?

FATHER
I don't want to frighten you!

WILFRID
Now I'm really losing my mind! This can't be happening! I'm not dreaming, I'm awake, I'm not dreaming!

FATHER
No, you're not dreaming.

WILFRID
So then, what are you doing here?

FATHER
What do you mean, what am I doing here?

WILFRID
I mean, you're dead. You're dead, right? You're dead?

FATHER
You always complicate everything!

WILFRID
I must be dreaming! I'm dreaming!

FATHER
Why are you getting so upset?

WILFRID
Because you're dead! That's why I'm getting so upset!

FATHER
But there's no reason to get upset. I'm dead, I'm dead, but it's not the end of the world. The proof: I'm here, with you, we're both here, and we're together and that's all right. And that's it.

WILFRID
But it's not normal. It's totally weird!

FATHER
What do you mean, it's weird!

WILFRID
I mean, the fact that you're here with me, sitting here calmly! The

dead are the dead and the living are the living. But you dead with me living – that's weird.

FATHER
What's weird about it?

WILFRID
Well, nothing, except that I'm freaking out just a bit, I don't know what's going on anymore, I don't know if I'm dreaming anymore, I don't know if I'm asleep anymore, I don't even know if I'm still alive. I don't even know who's dead anymore! Who's dead, huh? Which of the two of us is dead? Maybe it's me, if I'm here with you it's because I'm dead, maybe you're the one who's alive and you just lost your son, your son is dead, he's dead!

FATHER
No, you're not dead. If you were dead, you'd know it, you wouldn't have the slightest doubt. Believe me, I know from experience.

WILFRID
Maybe! But I don't understand why you came. You're scaring me, yes, you're scaring me! And I'm trying to do my best to bury you with Mom, but it isn't easy!

FATHER
I know. But that's not why I came to see you, Wilfrid.

WILFRID
Then why did you?

FATHER
I saw that you opened my little red suitcase. And I wanted to be with you to help you understand a bit what's in it.

WILFRID
What's in it?

FATHER
Look.

WILFRID
"Unsent letters." What's that?

FATHER
Unsent letters, letters I never sent.

WILFRID
Wilfrid, Wilfrid, Wilfrid, Wilfrid, Wilfrid, Wilfrid… letters to me?

FATHER
If your name is on them, then they're to you. They tell you a bit about who your father was, and who your mother was.

—— 12. The Seashore ——

The FATHER is sitting at a table in a café. He writes the letter that WILFRID is reading.

ADULT FATHER
My little Wilfrid, I don't know why I'm writing to you, I don't know why I'm writing. I don't know who I am anymore. I'm writing to you because there's no one else to write to. Today is your second birthday, you're two years old and I weep when I think of how sad the days that mark your birth will be since that day will also remind you of your mother's death. You are two years old…

FATHER
…and I'm not with you, I can't be with you there in that strange country where I can never be at home. Who am I writing to? Why am I writing? Who will read my words? Who will console me? How can I go on living, my dear Wilfrid? I wish the three of us were all together, snuggled together, but look what life has done to us. But I don't want to be sad…

ADULT FATHER
… today you are two years old and I want you to keep a happy memory of your mother, and of your father, so for your second birthday my gift to you is my most beautiful memory since I have nothing better to give. It was on a beach and it was raining. We'd been dancing, the servants following us with umbrellas.

WILFRID
Servants? You had servants?

FATHER
Your mother's family was very rich. And your aunt, as a wedding gift, gave us two servants.

The YOUNG FATHER and JEANNE enter.

WILFRID
Is that you two?

FATHER
That's us.

WILFRID
You were beautiful.

FATHER
We were happy. When you're happy, it's easy to be beautiful. And then there was the sea, the wind and the rain. How can you not be beautiful when there's so much water around you?

YOUNG FATHER
There's a lot of water in our story!

HOUSEKEEPER
If Sir and Madam would like to go back to the house…

JEANNE
Sir and Madam don't want to go back.

SERVANT
The weather's turning.

YOUNG FATHER
Let it turn!

HOUSEKEEPER
The wind is rising.

JEANNE
Let it rise.

SERVANT
There's going to be a storm.

FATHER
I hope there'll be a storm.

YOUNG FATHER
I hope there'll be a storm.

HOUSEKEEPER
But we're all going to get soaked!

JEANNE
Go back quickly then, take your umbrellas with you and go!

SERVANT
But we can't leave you here, I mean, we're your servants.

JEANNE
Go back and get warmed up, that's an order. You're the servants and we're the masters. We can let ourselves get sick, but we can't let you. So hurry, go protect yourselves so you don't catch cold, that's an order.

SERVANT & HOUSEKEEPER
Very well, Madam.

ADULT FATHER
We were so happy, Wilfrid. Your aunts and uncles would watch us from a distance.

YOUNG FATHER
They're up there under their roofs, behind their windows, behind their shutters, watching us in the rain.

JEANNE
They're watching us. They're up there and they're watching us!

YOUNG FATHER
They must not be very happy.

JEANNE
They must be jealous!

YOUNG FATHER
Let's dance some more!

JEANNE
Make love to me.

WILFRID
What?

JEANNE
Make love to me! We'll have a child!

FATHER
You can't have a child, you know very well!

JEANNE
I can have a child and we will have a child.

YOUNG FATHER
The doctors said you're too fragile.

JEANNE
Doctors say anything. Do you know any woman who died giving birth? I don't. You don't die in childbirth anymore. We'll have a child. Don't you want a child?

YOUNG FATHER
Of course!

JEANNE
Fine. Then we'll have a child. And that's that.

WILFRID
How is it that I was born here?

FATHER
Go figure. Who knows. It all happened so fast. The war, the family, I don't know anymore, I don't know. Open it and read, you'll find out. I told you the whole story. All of it.

WILFRID
I don't know if I really want to know.

FATHER
Then who will want to know? No one knows this story. Two people loved each other, the woman died, the man went crazy. No one cares anymore.

WILFRID
It's not easy to be told a story where the hero dies at the end.

— 13. Bombing —

Neighbours appear on their balconies, worried. They call to each other. WILFRID opens another letter. A bomb explodes. Violently.

WILFRID
During the war, we lived on the sixth floor of an eight-story building and the apartments were one on top of the other.

FATHER
It gave us the feeling we were all living in each others' pockets. Aunt Marie lived on the seventh floor, Uncle Émile on the third, and the other floors were occupied by neighbours who we got to know from spending so much time in the same bomb shelter, which was in the basement.

JEANNE
Hello, Lucie, it's Jeanne, no, there's no bombing today, what about in your neighbourhood? Yes, I went to the doctor this morning, he said I couldn't keep the baby. *(bomb)* No no, it's just routine bombing. *(bomb)* No, I'm not alone, Thomas is here, he's at the window.

Bomb.

MOUSSA
Thomas.

YOUNG FATHER
Moussa.

MARIE
Thomas.

YOUNG FATHER
Marie.

MARIE
Moussa.

MOUSSA
Marie.

Bomb.

JEANNE
What?

MOUSSA & MARIE
What should we do?

YOUNG FATHER
Should we go down?

MOUSSA & MARIE
I don't know.

YOUNG FATHER
We'll go down.

MARIE
I'll meet you there.

MOUSSA
I'll go down to see what Émile's doing.

JEANNE
The doctor told me I can't keep the baby because I'm too fragile.

MOUSSA
Émile.

ÉMILE
Moussa.

MARIE
Jeanne!

JEANNE
Because I'm too fragile.

MARIE
We have to go to the basement.

JEANNE
No we don't, it's just routine bombing.

YOUNG FATHER
We're going down.

MARIE
We're going down.

MOUSSA
We'll meet you back up here later.

OLD WOMAN
Go down!

JEANNE
We want to keep the baby, I'm not even considering an abortion.

YOUNG FATHER
Jeanne, you'll call her back later, we're going down to the shelter.

JEANNE
I'll let you go, we're going down to the shelter, I'll call you later.

OLD WOMAN
Go downstairs!

They go downstairs and bombs are heard intermittently. They reach the shelter.

ÉMILE
All right, I'm going too.

ADULT FATHER
My dear Wilfrid,
I'm sitting in a café and I'm writing to you. Today is your tenth birthday. It's been ten years since your mother died. Yesterday I arrived by ship in this country of desert and sun, the people here have dark skin. I know someone who will give me work as a house painter. I think about your mother. Here I am, in the sun. I think of those happy days during the war. Your mother was alive. Bombs dropped and we played cards with the neighbours in a shelter. You were still in her belly. I would look at her and think about you, you kept me warm in the midst of that horror.

The bombing would disappear, everything would disappear except her laughter and you in her belly and life despite everything, still despite everything!

WILFRID
You wrote me letters for years without ever mailing a single one?

FATHER
That's right.

WILFRID
Why? Why did you write them if you knew you were never going to send them?

FATHER
I didn't know. I never knew. Each time I'd say to myself, this one I'll send, and then I'd end up carrying it around in my pocket, and then it would be too late.

WILFRID
Do you realize I never knew where you were, do you realize how proud I'd have been to say that my father was a travelling man, a poet on the great open seas of the world, a wanderer who sends me letters from the four corners of the earth to tell me how much he loved my mother?

FATHER
All those letters were so sad. So full of melancholy, Wilfrid, why would I have sent them?

WILFRID
So I'd have some idea what I meant to you. What I was to you. What was I? A son? A complete stranger? An unknown son who you left in the hands of my aunts who spent my whole childhood telling me all kinds of crazy things about you?

FATHER
People say whatever they want.

WILFRID
What was I to you?

FATHER
I can't tell you any more than those letters do.

WILFRID
So, Your Honour, I opened letter after letter to find, to understand, understand what? I read those letters and I knew that everything, from that moment, was going to slip away from me and dissolve. My whole life was spilling out of those envelopes I opened, my memory, my imagination, everything slipped away and dissolved, Your Honour. Where do I come from? What am I? Who am I? I suddenly had the overwhelming feeling that I wasn't me anymore, that there was another Wilfrid and that *that* Wilfrid was something I could almost see and touch. I have the feeling, Your Honour, that I'm watching a performance and that I'm watching myself. I see it clearly. Yes. All those letters my father wrote me, what were they but proof that I never really existed, since they weren't addressed to me but to someone other than me, another guy who's a lot like me, who's the same age, whose name is also Wilfrid, and who, by the most amazing coincidence, lives in my body? I spent the night poring over those letters, a lot of them talked about land, my father's country, childhood. Always about the sea, often the sea. With my mother. Sometimes they talked about death, often they talked about love. A lot about love.

—— 14. Love ——

JEANNE
Thomas.

ADULT FATHER
Jeanne.

JEANNE
Death is nothing because it gave you a son.

ADULT FATHER
But you're not here anymore.

FATHER
You're not here anymore.

JEANNE
I'm here in his eyes.

ADULT FATHER
I miss you so much.

JEANNE
Where are you now?

ADULT FATHER
I'm walking through the streets of a big city. I'm putting up posters.

JEANNE
And Wilfrid? What are you doing about your son, Thomas?

ADULT FATHER
I write to him.

JEANNE
Letters you never send him.

FATHER
Wilfrid is grown up now, he's twenty, he's getting along fine. I can't bear to see him, he'll remind me too much of you.

YOUNG FATHER
Jeanne!

JEANNE
Thomas!

FATHER
Yes, Jeanne.

ADULT FATHER
Yes, Jeanne.

JEANNE
It's you running along the beach, look, you're coming towards me.

YOUNG FATHER
Jeanne. What are you doing on the beach all alone? What are you doing? I was watching you from back there, you looked all dreamy, with ghosts all around you. Jeanne, I love you.

JEANNE
You even called me "my love."

YOUNG FATHER
I say the words "my love" like a prayer, because my love is already a prayer.

FATHER
Jeanne, let's stay like this forever, like the silhouette of a man on a stained glass window, facing the silhouette of a woman on another stained glass window, the shades of humanity, their icy steps echoing, passing between us.

YOUNG FATHER
I came to see you, Jeanne, here, in the midst of the wind coming off the sea, to ask you to marry me. There – I love you and these are things one doesn't speak aloud, but who cares, I'm saying them, I love you, don't say a word, the sea is speaking, she's speaking for you, I'm crazy because I'm standing with you here, in front of the sea, to pledge my love, my friendship, to pledge my loveship. Don't answer, don't say a word.

JEANNE
Look, Thomas, it's us, back when we wanted to do everything, be happy, happiness was at our feet, if you'd known, would you have loved me? If you'd known there would be the war, pain, death, would you have loved me the way you love me now?

FATHER
Forget, Jeanne, forget. Come back into my arms, yes, stay here and forget the future. I loved you, Jeanne, without pain, without war, without suffering, with love.

—— 15. Solitude ——

Back at WILFRID's apartment.

WILFRID
What were you doing sitting on the bench when they found you dead? What were you doing there?

FATHER
I was waiting for the sun to come up.

WILFRID
Why didn't you call me? Why didn't you come and ring my doorbell, why didn't you come?

FATHER
I *did* come. You weren't home.

WILFRID
Why didn't you wait for me?

FATHER
I *did* wait. Then, early in the night, I saw you come home. You were with a girl. I didn't want to disturb you. I know what that's like.

WILFRID
What do you know?

FATHER
I know what it's like to come home late with a girl. I may be dead, but I'm not an idiot.

WILFRID
So you knew. You knew what I was doing while you were dying.

FATHER
When you die, you don't know anything anymore, Wilfrid. You're nothing more than a poor dog, all alone in the eye of a storm. Have you ever seen a dog get pulled by the tide? When you die you become the dog, with a dog's terrified eyes, all alone in the middle of a huge wave that drags us towards the open sea. The open sea is terrifying when there's no horizon, so you shit and you piss because there's nothing else to do but shit and piss, like a final act of life, a final gesture to leave a trace before you're gone, our trace, our smell.

WILFRID
At the morgue they said you died of an aneurysm.

FATHER
At this point you wouldn't believe how little I care.

WILFRID tears open another letter.

—— 16. Mother and Son ——

JEANNE
Wilfrid.

WILFRID
Mom…

JEANNE
I'm trying to find your father's grave. Do you remember where he's buried?

WILFRID
But he hasn't been buried yet, that's exactly the problem.

JEANNE
How can he not have been buried, what are you talking about? Your father was buried here, in this cemetery. Look, I put on my wedding dress, your father died the day of my wedding. I brought someone with me who can play music, but I can't find the grave. But I was sure it was here.

WILFRID
No, you're the one who's buried here, in the family tomb.

JEANNE
The sea air is good.

WILFRID
What are you talking about? There's no sea anymore.

JEANNE
You can hear the waves, it's so good to hear the waves, panting and panting and panting, towards a climax that will never come. Your father's happy you've buried him here, on this beach.

WILFRID
Where exactly is here?

JEANNE
It's your father's country, your mother's country. We were born here. Your father's happy to be buried in his homeland. He never went back after I died.

FATHER
Jeanne.

JEANNE
You brought me a bouquet of flowers. You're crazy.

FATHER
Now that I'm dead, I can be a little crazy.

JEANNE throws the bouquet.

WILFRID
But I don't know where to bury Dad, I don't know.... You say he's buried here, over there, but he's not, he's still among the living, he isn't at rest, he isn't anything, Dad isn't buried anywhere and I don't know how to bury him, I don't know how one goes about burying one's father.

JEANNE
But no, he's here, your father is buried here, in this cemetery, on the seashore, in his homeland, and he's happy...

WILFRID
But he can't be buried here because he died thousands of kilometres from this shore!

JEANNE
Wilfrid, your father is a keeper of flocks.

WILFRID
What??!

JEANNE
Your father is a keeper of flocks.

WILFRID wakes up.

WILFRID
I'd fallen asleep reading the letter. And the letter I was holding wasn't a letter, Your Honour, but a photograph of my mother and father at the seaside in their country. Look, Your Honour. It's them. When I woke up, I had only that phrase in my head: "Your father is a keeper of flocks," and I didn't understand. Dawn was breaking. I'd opened all the letters. I'd learned a lot of things, but what did it ultimately mean? Nothing. That I was an orphan now. One more orphan. Like you, like a lot of people, and, like a lot of people no doubt, I was trying to find an explanation, something that my rational mind could cling to so I could understand what had happened. Because I, Wilfrid, had lost my father and mother. But there's nothing to understand except maybe that there are things that happen and leave us forever inconsolable. So I went

back to the funeral parlour in the morning. There was no one there. I didn't bother with my nice suit, and put on the jacket he was wearing when they found him. In the inside pocket I found another letter addressed to me. His last. It was dated two days earlier, that is, the very day my father died.

—— 17. Pain and childbirth ——

WILFRID reads.

FATHER
Wilfrid, how old are you? How old? I don't remember any-more.... Today must be your birthday but I'm not sure anymore, I'm not sure about anything. My memory is a forest. Your mother's the only one who walks through it. Her footsteps rummage through my brain and keep bringing memory back to life. My head is full of dead leaves that rustle under the feet of your dead mother. Now I am nothing more than a traveller on the road between what I'm forgetting and the endless creaking of my brain. How can death bring forth life? My memory is a forest where trees are being felled. I'm forgetting....

JEANNE screams.

ALL THREE FATHERS
Jeanne!

DOCTOR
We're losing her...

JEANNE
Don't keep me here, don't hold me here.

YOUNG FATHER
Jeanne, don't leave!

DOCTOR
We're losing her...

JEANNE
I feel him in my belly, I feel him.

YOUNG FATHER
Save her, doctor, save her!

DOCTOR
Sir, we're losing her. If you want to save her, we have to sacrifice the child.

YOUNG FATHER
Sacrifice the child.

JEANNE
No! Save the child! Save the child!

YOUNG FATHER
Go on, doctor!

JEANNE
Thomas, you promised me.

YOUNG FATHER
Forget the child!

JEANNE
No! No, Thomas, Thomas, you promised me, you promised me…

YOUNG FATHER
Jeanne!

JEANNE
You promised a thousand times, a thousand times that it would be him, never me…

YOUNG FATHER
Yes, I promised, I promised, but it's not possible, Jeanne.

JEANNE
I feel him there. Beating…

YOUNG FATHER
I can't, Jeanne, I can't…

JEANNE
For you, for me, he'll be both of us, both of us in him, we'll leave life a gift, without him, no more life, no more anything, nothing, you promised, you promised Thomas, you promised…

YOUNG FATHER
Jeanne!

DOCTOR
What do you want us to do?

JEANNE
I feel him deep inside me, a pain that gives life meaning, he's there, he's there, Thomas, please, I'm begging you…

YOUNG FATHER
Save her.

JEANNE
He's slipping out of me, he's sliding, I feel him sliding, what light is spilling out of my depths, what light, what sweetness is freeing itself from me, escaping, evaporating, I'm slipping towards a light that's piercing right through me!

DOCTOR
Make a decision sir, or we'll lose them both!

JEANNE
Thomas, think of me, don't think about yourself! Forget your heartbreak, never mind your grief! Be strong, Thomas, be strong!

DOCTOR
Tell us now!

YOUNG FATHER
Save the child.

JEANNE
What flavour is drawing me? What unknown land am I rising towards? It's the whole of life that's sliding out of me.

YOUNG FATHER
Jeanne.

JEANNE
It's here, life is here!

YOUNG FATHER
Jeanne.

JEANNE
Life is so beautiful.

JEANNE dies.

FATHER

Did I do the right thing, Wilfrid? Did I do the right thing? I've been obsessed with this question ever since – it's haunted me. It's a very fast question, I couldn't outrun it; no train, no plane could ever manage to shake it; at the farthest corner of the world, in the darkest streets of the darkest towns, it always managed to find me again. I can't even tell anymore if all that really happened, but you're here to remind me that my life wasn't a dream, that a long time ago I committed an act that turned my life upside down. Did I do the right thing? Your mother's family says I'm a murderer. They may be right. Whether or not they are, Wilfrid, I was happy in my country. In my country I loved your mother, in my country I knew happiness, and thanks to you, thanks to your mother, my life won't have been a total waste.

—— 18. Request ——

WILFRID and the MAGISTRATE.

WILFRID

My request is simple, Your Honour. I ask for the right to bury my father's body in his homeland. I know my father wasn't a Chief of State or a public figure, but for me, it might be a way to reconcile things. The dead with the living. The living suffer, but the dead are important too. The dead are eternal, you know, so we just have to help them rest in peace, because they're going to have to rest for a long time and eternity is long, Your Honour. Here, my father would be in a very awkward situation. My father didn't live here, Your Honour, my father's love is over there, his happiness is over there, and a bit of me comes from over there as well. Your Honour, everything's ready, I've purchased everything, the plane tickets, everything, I'm ready, the funeral home is ready to help me, they'll transport the body to the airport for a minimal fee, I'm all organized to leave tonight. Over there I know where to go, to my father's village, high in the mountains, all I need is your authorization, Your Honour, so that I can make this journey, that's all. I've told you everything.

The film crew enters.

DIRECTOR

Don't turn back, Wilfrid. Today you're going to undertake a journey that will lead you to your father's land.

WILFRID

Are you coming, Dad?

THE FATHER

Where are we going?

WILFRID

I'm taking you home.

DIRECTOR

Wilfrid, without knowing it, you've just stepped off the path to throw yourself headfirst into the abyss.

OVER THERE

— 19. The blind man who reads in the middle of the night —

Night. The sound of a violin in the distance.

ULRICH
Sing, Goddess, Achilles' maniac rage: ruinous thing! It roused a thousand sorrows and hurled many souls of mighty warriors to Hades, made their bodies food for dogs and carrion birds.... Sing, Goddess, the sorrow of aged Priam at the feet of Achilles son of Peleus, begging him to return the corpse of his son Hector...

SIMONE
(shouting into the distance) At the crossroads, we might meet the Other!

ULRICH
And I'm the blind man who reads in the middle of the night! Keep shouting, Simone, keep shouting!
Remember your father, Achilles, respect the Gods, and listen to my lament. I had a son who guarded our people and our city – yesterday you slew him. It was Hector. He's the reason I've come today to the Achaen ships to claim his remains. Respect the Gods, Achilles, have pity on me for your father's sake.
Listen, someone's coming! I hear the walker's footsteps.... A strange walker... his step is weak, he's just passed the village fountain, I hear him climbing the mountain, he's coming towards me. He's even staggering!

WILFRID
(in the distance) Ha! Shit!

FATHER
(in the distance) The music was coming from over there...

ULRICH
He's not very happy! I don't recognize his footsteps. Those aren't Simone's footsteps! No. A visitor. Or perhaps a lost traveller. He's coming this way.

FATHER
The music was coming from here.

WILFRID

I know the music was coming from here. But there's no more music now, so I don't have a clue where we are. It's as dark as a bear's asshole, I can't see a thing and I'm tired, so you know what you're going to do, Dad?

FATHER

What?

WILFRID

You're going to play dead. That is, you're going to shut up and leave me alone for a while.

FATHER

You aren't being very nice, Wilfrid.

WILFRID

I don't care, I'm wiped and I don't know where I am. I'm not having an easy time. If you want to make me happy, go back to your corpse and wait for me there. When I've figured out how to bury you, I'll come back and get you.

FATHER

Since you're asking me so nicely, I'll go back to my corpse. But you seem to have forgotten I'm in the village where I was born that I haven't seen for twenty-six years, and if you'd put yourself in my shoes for a moment you'd understand.

WILFRID

Dad!

FATHER

All right, All right, I'm going, forget it!

WILFRID

But *I'm* not the one who needs to understand! You're dead, you can afford not to give a damn, but my feet hurt, my legs hurt, and I have a headache!!

ULRICH

Who are you?

WILFRID

Ah! Good God… I didn't see you!

ULRICH
Funny, *I'm* supposed to be the blind one.

WILFRID
Well, I still didn't see you. It's so dark.

ULRICH
Who are you?

WILFRID
My name is Wilfrid.

ULRICH
What village are you from?

WILFRID
I'm not from a village, I'm from very far away. I've crossed an ocean.

FATHER
Wilfrid, ask him his name. His face rings a bell.

ULRICH
And what brings you here in the middle of the night?

WILFRID
It may seem a bit obscure to you.

ULRICH
That's fine, I'm used to being in the dark. What do you want, Wilfrid? Forgive my curiosity, but we never see strangers around here.

WILFRID
It's true that I'm a stranger, but my father's from this village.

ULRICH
Your father?

WILFRID
His name is Thomas.

ULRICH
There's no Thomas in the village.

WILFRID
I know.

ULRICH
Explain.

WILFRID
Where should I begin?

ULRICH
That's always the question.

WILFRID
What's your name?

ULRICH
Ulrich!

WILFRID
You don't remember Thomas?

ULRICH
Thomas…? no.

WILFRID
What about Jeanne, then, who he was married to?

FATHER
Show him the photo!

WILFRID
He's blind, Dad!

ULRICH
Jeanne…. No, I don't see. A girl from the village?

WILFRID
No, she was from the sea, but they lived here for a while, I think.

ULRICH
I might have known them. But a long time ago.

WILFRID
She was beautiful.

ULRICH
That's vague. I only see through my fingers.

WILFRID
The day the country was invaded, they fled.

ULRICH
A lot of people fled back then.

WILFRID
Yes, but they were able to go far away, very far, not just to the other end of the country, but even further, to faraway lands.

ULRICH
Tell me more.

WILFRID
I don't know any more.

FATHER & JEANNE
Tell him about the sea.

WILFRID
They would go for walks right to the sea.

ULRICH
A man and a woman… such a long time ago…

FATHER
He's remembering!

ULRICH
They would leave every Saturday in their Sunday best. Outfits that blared whiteness in the sunlight. That sometimes pierced the darkness of my brain. They would come back laughing. I would hear them.

WILFRID
You remember?

ULRICH
Thomas and Jeanne. *(ULRICH touches WILFRID's face.)* What sudden clamour is rising in me, like the call of the past, the call of what has long been forgotten? And you are their son, the child

she was carrying in her belly. The night you were conceived, hate rained down on the village. The very night the great oak died, ravaged by a bomb. I heard it shriek. Crows threw themselves into the cliff. They were found in the morning, their skulls fractured, their hearts burst, their feathers full of blood.

WILFRID
You're trembling!

ULRICH
I'm trembling, Yes. I feel, yes I feel that all of a sudden a distant star moved a few inches closer to us to make us understand that our lives will change. What have you come here for, Wilfrid, son of Thomas? Where are your parents?

WILFRID
They're dead. I've come here with my father's body. My father died three days ago, and I've come to bury him in his village, to help him make peace with life. And I need help. The body's much too heavy.

ULRICH
I'm afraid he'll soon seem even heavier.

WILFRID
What do you mean?

ULRICH
Because here, in this village, there's no more room to bury anyone. Three days ago, a child died. To bury him, we had to dig up a coffin and bury the child's body with a skeleton whitened by worms.

WILFRID
Come on, there has to be room for one more!

SIMONE
(in the distance) At the crossroads, we might meet the Other!

WILFRID
What's that?!

ULRICH
Simone who plays her violin in the distance and who makes all the villagers furious. You've come to a strange country, Wilfrid.

Here people are bitter, they don't want to hear anything, not music, not anything – not children's cries, nor their rage. The old people are old around here and they want calm, but Simone shouts her lungs out, in the middle of the night, and plays constantly to break the calm, because Simone doesn't care, Simone is skinny, Simone is ugly, Simone is alone, Simone is full of rage and she plays her violin!

SIMONE
(in the distance) At the crossroads, we might meet the Other!

ULRICH
And she shouts! And they are furious! *And* they're on their way here. You'll see, they're pretty stuck in the past. But you mustn't hold it against them, they suffered a lot during the war.

—— 20. Villagers ——

SIMONE
(in the distance) Is there anyone who'd like to hear me say "here I am?"

FARID
Ulrich, this time we've got to put a stop to it! Do you hear her play and shout? We can't get any sleep anymore! Where is she hiding?

ULRICH
I'm blind, my good Farid.

ANKIA
Simone often keeps you company!

ULRICH
She reads me books. She is my eyes.

JOSEPH
You know what she did two days ago?

ANKIA
During little Saïd's funeral, she played music that could break your heart.

FARID
So why does she keep playing when all of those who've lost a son or daughter ask her to throw her instrument into the fire.

ULRICH
Because she's angry. Simone is angry.

The violin music starts up again. In the distance, very slow, very beautiful.

FARID
Listen to her. She's mocking us! It's obvious! In the middle of the night.

SIMONE
(in the distance) At the crossroads, we might meet the Other!

ANKIA
She's calling the trees, she's talking to them, telling them to flee, she's a lunatic! Listen!

JOSEPH
Yesterday, not far from the blue boulder, and near the grottos where the elders used to hide, Klamm found more bottles with paper in them, in the river that runs down to the other villages, paper with symbols, words, dates!

ULRICH
Listen to the music and you'll understand Simone. Who's the blind one here? Who?

ISSAM
You're protecting her, you old fool, you're protecting her when she's keeping the whole village awake, when the whole village is exhausted, ruined by a nightmare without a name, when our land has been conquered, invaded, overrun by others, the enemy has won, our country no longer bears its true name, and you, you're protecting her, she's trying to console us for something we can never be consoled for!

ANKIA
The music's getting closer!

FARID
She's coming back!

—— 21. Simone ——

SIMONE

Last night it rained.

ANKIA

Simone! Everyone's been looking for you!

ISSAM

Stop playing your instrument! How many times do we have to tell you?

SIMONE

I don't know what you're talking about, I don't even know who you are, but I know one thing, that I'm not you; and I don't care about you in any case. About your customs, your rituals, your bullshit rules and regulations! I'm not playing for you, I've never played for you! You're old and ugly. I don't care what you think of me, I don't care what you say about me, I don't know you, I'm not you!

ISSAM

Who are you then? With the phrases you shout in the night and the words you throw down the river in a bottle, who are you? What are you doing? What are you looking for? Stupid girl, you stupid idiot, don't you understand that it's all over?

SIMONE

But not that long ago you promised me that the war was a bad thing that had to disappear, that had to end so that freedom could finally be born. Now the war is over and I'm still in prison. You're still telling me not to play, not to speak, not to dream. You tell me to shut up, Simone, shut up! You're liars.

ALL EXCEPT ULRICH

Shut up!

SIMONE

I won't stop insulting you till you shut your mouths. QUIET! Listen to my violin, listen! It's music to remind the living of the dead. Listen!

FARID

Saïd is dead, the last son has just left the village. And you, you were playing your instrument?

SIMONE
Saïd loved music. He often came to listen to me!

ISSAM
What an insult to his parents, to the sorrow they're suffering! What an insult!

FARID
Stop playing!

SIMONE
Give me back my violin!

FARID
We should break your violin.

SIMONE
Give me back my violin!

ANKIA
Yes, we should break it so that you'll understand once and for all that you aren't living alone, that the village doesn't belong to you and that there are customs and practices you have to respect!

SIMONE
Give me back my violin!

ISSAM
We won't give you back your violin. You're a little girl whose parents had no time to raise properly before they died and you've taken advantage of the war to do whatever you feel like, but today that's over, you're going to calm down, you're going to sit down and shut up and do what you're told!

SIMONE
Give me back my violin!

ISSAM
Here, here's your violin!

ISSAM slaps SIMONE.

ULRICH
That's enough! Give her back her violin.

ISSAM
Here, take it. Let's go.

—— 22. Encounter ——

SIMONE
Ulrich, it's true that there are no children in the village. The jaws of death have ransacked the whole country. There's no one my age to play with, or talk with!

ULRICH
In the villages, down in the valley, there must be some.

SIMONE
Maybe not. For months I've been sending tons of messages, building a resistance cell. I've tossed tons of bottles into the dark river, the one that goes down to the villages below. Nothing. Nobody answers me. Who are the others, Ulrich, who are they? Even yesterday, I was sure that in all the villages there are people like me who want to find each other, who are bored, who are searching, who are sick of always hearing people talk about the same thing, all the time, all the time.

ULRICH
So?

SIMONE
So nothing. I don't know. I have the feeling I'm all alone in the middle of this mountain. I want to get outside of myself, Ulrich, I want to get away from myself and meet someone, someone with a different face than mine, the face of another, the other, Ulrich, the other. The whole storyline of life is born through our encounter with the other, but there's no one here, there's no one. The bottles I send, the signals I play with my violin, the phrases I shout get lost in the night, always. Never any answer, never! Sometimes I sit in unfamiliar places, for a long, long time and I wait for someone to come, but no one comes, there are only the trees, only the trees!

ULRICH
You're looking for a miracle, Simone.

SIMONE
We all need a miracle. You old people, you had your miracle a long time ago, because you knew the country before the war, but I was born in the midst of bombing, yet I'm sure that life is something other than bombs, that it can be something else, but I don't know what.

ULRICH
Did you send any messages today?

SIMONE
This morning I got three bottles ready to throw into the river.

ULRICH
Go back to the cliff, Simone, the one overlooking the village below, and shout as loud as you can that Wilfrid has returned. Shout that Thomas is dead. Shout that he has the right to a burial place.

SIMONE
What are you talking about, Ulrich?

ULRICH
Simone, the answer you were waiting for has come, but you can't hear it, you can't recognize it, because it's coming from the side you were least expecting. Simone, this is Wilfrid.

SIMONE
I haven't seen people my age for a long time.

ULRICH
Wilfrid, this is Simone. I think you two need each other.

SIMONE
Are you coming? We're going to wake everyone up.

WILFRID
I need help to bring my father's body up here.

SIMONE
I'll help you.

WILFRID
And what will we do about the burial place?

ULRICH

Tomorrow morning we'll talk with the villagers, maybe someone will have an idea where to find him a spot. They must remember your father. Good night, Simone, shout loudly, so that everybody hears. Shout that the miracle has come. And then you'll come and tell me what happened.

—— 23. In the dark ——

The FATHER is walking around. WILFRID and SIMONE are looking for him.

FATHER

Wilfrid, I don't want to clutter up your head, but I don't have any other place to go and get warmed up. Even dead, death frightens me, just like when I was alive, life frightened me. It takes a certain amount of time to get used to it. I swear to you Wilfrid, I won't stay and haunt your dreams for long, but let me take up all the space in your life for just a little while, just till I get used to the idea of being dead. Now that I'm dead, I can only express my great astonishment. I'm dead and I just can't believe it.

WILFRID

Here.

SIMONE

We'll bring him over to the cliff first. *(They carry the FATHER.)* Now, repeat after me. *(She shouts.)* "Wilfrid is here! Thomas is dead. Here I am."

WILFRID & SIMONE

"Here I am. Here I am. The miracle has come."

WILFRID

Look down there!

SIMONE

It's the lower village.

WILFRID

A light went on.

SIMONE
It's been turning on the last few nights. But I don't know if it turns on for me or for no reason.

WILFRID
It just went off.

SIMONE
It always goes off.

WILFRID
Tomorrow you should go see.

SIMONE
I know but I'm afraid, the day I set foot outside the village I'll never come back. Tomorrow we have to take care of your father's body. If it's really for me, the light will still be there the next few nights.

WILFRID
Should we leave the body here?

SIMONE
We'll carry it to the town square. When they see it, the villagers will take pity on him. Come, I'll introduce you to them.

—— 24. Village Square ——

The villagers are gathered around WILFRID and SIMONE.

ISSAM
We remember your father very well. He was a man who let himself be misled, and who aspired to a situation beyond his station. Look at you, you were able to get out because of your wife's money, but you died before all of us who stayed behind. Coward!

FATHER
Screw you, asshole.

WILFRID
Dad!

FATHER
What? He can't hear me.

ISSAM
Having his body here doesn't interest us, and we can't understand why you brought it all the way here to show us.

WILFRID
I obviously didn't bring it all the way here just to show you, but I wanted, to help him kind of make peace with life, to bury him in the village he was born in. Here, I mean.

ISSAM
That's a good one!

ANKIA
Very funny!

FARID
Hilarious!

JOSEPH
You can say that again!

ISSAM
So you're saying you want to bury him here.

WILFRID
Yes.

ISSAM
Just like that!

WILFRID
Yes, just like that!

ISSAM
That's a good one!

ANKIA
Very funny!

FARID
Hilarious!

JOSEPH
You can say that again!

ANKIA
Stupid boy! How could you have known? The cemetery is bursting at the seams. There's no room left.

SIMONE
Hold on a minute! There must be some tiny little corner where we can bury him, at the edge of a field, or in the middle of an abandoned lot!

ISSAM
The lots and fields are full of landmines. So many people have been blown to bits just wandering through, you know that. As far as other places, they're reserved for people of the village, not strangers!

SIMONE
But he isn't a stranger! He was born here. You knew him!

ISSAM
He fled the country. He should have gotten himself buried somewhere else, wherever he went to.

SIMONE
You have no right to do that! You can't refuse hospitality to the dead. You don't have the right to keep the dead with the living!

ISSAM
What do you want, Simone? A man comes back and we should throw ourselves at his feet? You're too young, you're the youngest in the whole village and the youngest ones never grow up, they never understand anything! Do you think, Simone, that we enjoy refusing to bury a dead man? We don't. But we've been defeated and now, each one of us thinks about saving himself and that's all right. There's no room for anyone else.

JOSEPH
You could go see Hakim. He's rich, he has a large piece of property.

SIMONE
No, not Hakim, he won't understand a thing. He's a madman.

ISSAM
Well, you never know. Hakim's rich. He opened a cemetery in his garden. He's a businessman. He charges quite a bit for his plots.

ANKIA
But people say he might also give someone a plot for free if he's in a good mood.

WILFRID
What else is there to do? We're not exactly going to burn him! I haven't made this whole trip just to burn him!

SIMONE
Let's go, Wilfrid.

ANKIA
Take the corpse with you. We've smelled so much death during the war, I don't want to smell that stench any more.

—— 25. Torment ——

The film crew enters.

DIRECTOR
Excellent! The next scene is a big emotional scene! *(to SIMONE)* Now you, young lady, you stand here. It's windy, it's raining, it's hailing! Wilfrid! Where's Wilfrid!? Ah! There you are! Someone get the old man from his trailer! Now, Wilfrid you lean on the little girl, don't be afraid, she won't break! *(to the FATHER)* Hello sir!

FATHER
Hello!

DIRECTOR
You're here in your son's arms! It's hard, it's excruciating! Standing by!

SOUND PERSON
Sound rolling!

CAMERA PERSON
Camera rolling!

SCRIPT SUPERVISOR
Inner storm in the midst of torment, take one.

DIRECTOR
Stand by! Three two one…! *Action*! Wilfrid, here you are, sitting right in the middle of the road. Stand up and try to understand.

WILFRID
Understand what?

DIRECTOR
That you won't have any rest until your father is laid to rest.

WILFRID
I'd love to lay him to rest, but I don't know how!

DIRECTOR
Stop complaining! Stand up; the road to take is clear.

WILFRID
It may be clear but I can't see it!

SIMONE
We'll go see Hakim, maybe he'll help us.

WILFRID
You don't sound convinced!

SIMONE
I don't like that man. But we have no choice. Hakim is rich and he has a lot of land. We'll go during the evening meal. He's sure to be there.

WILFRID and SIMONE on the road.

We're here. Look, they're at the table.

— 26. Meal —

A group of rich people sitting at a table, eating.

JAMIL
Sir, we have visitors.

HAKIM
Who is it?

SIMONE
It's me, Mr. Hakim.

HAKIM
Our little musician! Speak of the devil! And who's this gentleman?

SIMONE
This is Wilfrid, a friend.

HAKIM
A friend! Jamil, two chairs for these young people!

JAMIL
Very well sir.

HAKIM
Where was I…?

MADAME HAKIM
The head.

GHASSANE
The head, yes, the head.

GUEST
The head.

HAKIM
Ah yes, the head. So, the head was in, the rest followed, and I could feel my balls slap against that whore's buttocks! *(burst of laughter from the others)* My time was up, I'd been banging away like a horny dog for the last two hours, but I didn't care, I had money—hell, I still do—and I told her: Keep it up, keep it up girlie, I have money and I don't give a fuck, though actually, I was giving her the fuck of her life, I was gripping her hips and hrnph hrnph hrnph, I started banging even harder, I felt my cock swell, a few more thrusts, then I fired my filthy rich jism right up her ass!

GHASSANE
Wonderful! Delectable.

HAKIM
Jamil, another bottle.

JAMIL
Yes, sir.

HAKIM
So, young people, how do they do it where you come from? Upside down? Rightside up? From the front or from behind?

SIMONE
Excuse us Mister Hakim, but I think we'll come back and see you tomorrow, when you've finished celebrating.

HAKIM
I won't hear of it! You're going to stay here and you're going to play a bit for us on your instrument!

ALL THE OTHERS
Oh yes, great idea, oh yes, really… yes…

SIMONE
No, I haven't come to play music, I didn't want to bother you, I didn't know you were dining with friends.

HAKIM
Sit down! Jamil, sit them back down! So tell me what brings you here, to what we owe the honour of this visit.

SIMONE
Wilfrid's father died. His father's name is Thomas, maybe you knew him, he lived in the village a long time ago. Now Wilfrid has returned his father's body to this country and he's looking for a place to bury him. We were told your property is large and that you might be able to help us!

HAKIM
Who said that?

SIMONE
The villagers.

HAKIM
They tell everyone anything they feel like!

MADAME HAKIM
They certainly do! One day–

HAKIM
Shut your face darling, shut the fuck up! And you came to see me about a burial place.

SIMONE
That's right.

WILFRID
Is it yes or no?

HAKIM
The young man's in a hurry.... *(the others laugh)* It's yes!

MADAME HAKIM
What do you mean, yes–

HAKIM
Shut your face darling, shut the fuck up.... But I'd like to see the body first.

WILFRID
What do you mean, see the body?

HAKIM
I'd simply like to know exactly what I'm going to bury in my garden! I'd like to see the body.

WILFRID
Never mind, we'll make other arrangements.

HAKIM
Other arrangements!

WILFRID
Yes!

HAKIM
Throughout the village they're killing each other to hold onto their spots, that bit of land where they can be put in the ground

and laid to rest, and you want to make other arrangements! All I'm asking is to see the body! I'm not asking you for a cent. *(The others laugh.)* Where is it?

WILFRID

Outside!

HAKIM

Outside? There's a corpse at my front door? That's wonderful! Go and get it... Jamil, go give them a hand.

WILFRID

Never mind, he's already here!

ALL EXCEPT WILFRID, SIMONE & JAMIL

My God, what a stench!

HAKIM

God he stinks!

WILFRID

He's dead, what do you expect!

GHASSANE

Can we touch him?

HAKIM

He looks like shit.

MADAME HAKIM

It's still a horrible smell! Has he been dead for very long?

WILFRID

All right, you've seen him, can we go now?

HAKIM

Take it easy, first we're going to honour the house with his presence, we're going to dance with the body.

WILFRID

Not a chance!

SIMONE

Listen sir, I think you're a little drunk and you don't know what you're doing!

HAKIM
I do what I want in my house. I'm not doing anything wrong, I want to honour my house, come and help me.

They dance with the body.

HAKIM
Dance, my friends, dance! Make him drink! He's earned it!

SIMONE
Stop that, stop it, all right!

HAKIM
It reminds me of the story of a friend who died a horrible death. A year or two ago, he was captured by the enemy with his 8-year-old daughter. They stripped him naked and they greased his asshole and sat him on a long wooden stake. It seems that it's an incredible caress that immediately puts you at attention in spite of yourself, and since there's no exception to the rule, as soon as they slid the stake up his ass he got a hard on, then they hoisted up his little girl, they spread her legs and they impaled her good and hard on her father's cock, and since she was wriggling like crazy as she screamed, her father slid up and down the pole groaning. In the end, the soldiers took pity on them and shot them both in the head right as he shot his wad into his daughter's ass.

WILFRID
STOP! AAAAAaaaaaaaaaaAAAAAAAAAH!!!!

KNIGHT
AAAAAaaaaaaaaaaAAAAAAAAAH!!!!

WILFRID & KNIGHT
AAAAAaaaaaaaaaaAAAAAAAAAH!!!!

They flee with the father.

WILFRID
Where the hell were we just now? Where were we Simone, where the hell were we? Oh, I'm feeling murderous, I feel like I could kill someone!

FATHER
Calm down, Wilfrid, calm down!

WILFRID
Nobody tell me to calm down! Okay?! I have no desire and no reason to calm down okay?! If you tell me one more time to calm down Dad, I'll kill you again, I don't want to calm down, I do not want to calm down one bit, I want… I want… I don't know what I want… I'm losing it, I'm fucking losing it, I'm losing it! AAAAh! I'm sick of it, I don't see the end, I don't see the end of anything! Not the end of the end of the end of the end of hell! I can't calm down, I'm not physically capable, I can't do it anymore… I can't take it anymore…. What are we going to do, Simone?

SIMONE
We'll go see Ulrich. To say goodbye to him.

ULRICH
Listen to what the star says, to what your pitiless star is telling you.

WILFRID
What is it saying?

ULRICH
Keep moving forward, even if you no longer believe. Keep going even when you've lost sight of your goal, keep going even when reason paralyzes you, even when you discover the futility of what going forward really means. Keep going even if you've lost all pride, all ability to hope. Keep moving forward.

—— 27. Curse ——

The KNIGHT, the FATHER, WILFRID and SIMONE sitting with ULRICH.

ULRICH
I've never seen the night, but people say that it's dark. So leave, leave – both of you, go before daybreak. In the morning I'll tell them all that the girl who played music has gone, I'll tell them that the young man who came back to his ancestral land has gone. I'll curse them, I'll tell them: Listen to the anger of youth that will make you the vanquished of the vanquished. Youth is

furious with you. Youth is leaving and the sun is leaving with her, I'll tell them not to seek the sun anymore, that the sun will return but never for them, that soon a thick fog will rise, a fog that will be the long tongue of death that will swallow them and suck them into the huge belly of death, death, who will spill its metal-corroding acids onto their bloody skulls and consume them. Simone, Wilfrid, take the body and leave before dawn. In the morning I'll tell them you've gone and that misfortune has just struck the village.

SIMONE

Ulrich, this melody will express my friendship for you better than words.

She plays.

WILFRID

Simone, look, the light from the lower village went on and off again.

SIMONE

Let's go. At dawn we'll be at the crossroads. Maybe the light will be there then.

THE OTHER

—— 28. The Crossroads ——

Dawn. At the crossroads. A young man is there.

AMÉ
Are you the night musician, the one who lives in the upper village?

SIMONE
I am. Are you the one who turned the light on?

AMÉ
I am.

SIMONE
What's your name?

AMÉ
Amé. Every night I heard your calls. And sometimes I found bottles with bits of paper in them. Messages. And everything talked about the crossroads. That at the crossroads, we could meet the other. So for days I've been coming here, to the crossroads. I wanted to know.

SIMONE
My name is Simone. This is Wilfrid. He's carrying his father's corpse.

AMÉ
What do you want?

SIMONE
I don't know. I was sick of everything. Aren't *you* sick of everything too?

AMÉ
Me? It's a miracle I haven't shot myself in the head.

SIMONE
Then stay with me.

AMÉ
What do you want to do?

SIMONE
First, find a place to bury the body, then leave.

AMÉ
Leave?

SIMONE
Yes, leave, go away, leave to learn about others. I can't stand hearing the old people anymore. Don't you hear them?

AMÉ
I see them! In the village, they're afraid of me, afraid I'll kill them, they know I've already killed, so of course they're afraid. They spy on me out of the corner of their eyes when I walk past, afraid I'll slit their throats, that I'll swallow them, that I'll chew up their hearts.

SIMONE
Do you want to come with me?

AMÉ
Where would we go?

SIMONE
To see if there are others like us, people our age, who'd also like to kill everybody… we'll go together and then I don't know…

AMÉ
We'll plant bombs.

SIMONE
Good idea.

AMÉ
During the war, I planted bombs.

SIMONE
Listen to me, the bomb I want to plant is even worse than the worst bomb that ever exploded in this country.

AMÉ
We'll plant them in buses, in restaurants…

SIMONE
No no, this bomb can only explode in a single place.

AMÉ
Where's that?

SIMONE
In people's heads.

AMÉ
In people's heads?

SIMONE
Yes.

AMÉ
What do you mean?

SIMONE
We'll go tell them stories. Stories that will force them to either tear our faces off or to come with us!

AMÉ
What kind of stories?

SIMONE
Our stories. Each of us will tell our own story.

AMÉ
But people don't give a shit about our stories! They especially don't care about yours. They say: too many stories, enough stories, no more stories. We'll blow things up instead!

SIMONE
Well anyway I'm leaving. First I'm going to help Wilfrid find a place to bury his father, then I'm leaving, and one way or another I'll find a way to tell people what happened, then they'll see, they'll know they weren't the only ones, that they're not alone. Are you coming?

AMÉ
I'm coming.

SIMONE
Your parents?

AMÉ
Dead.

SIMONE
Let's go.

AMÉ
No, not that way.

SIMONE
Yes, let's go to your village, we need to find somewhere to bury the body.

AMÉ
Forget the village. The dead have taken up all the space. Let's bury it here.

WILFRID
Here?

SIMONE
We can't bury him here.

AMÉ
Then over there. There, in the ditch.

WILFRID
Listen buddy, I know where you're coming from – even I get tempted to throw him in the first garbage can that comes along, but I also figure that if I've brought him this far, it's to find him somewhere decent.

AMÉ
But there isn't a decent place anywhere in the country. Get a grip. You're being such a jerk about your father's corpse! It's obvious that you've come from far away, otherwise, you wouldn't be so precious about it. Your father reeks and you have to bury him, period!

WILFRID
Hey! I didn't ask for your opinion. All I know is that burying him here is out of the question!

AMÉ
Fine. See ya, I'll leave you two with your little burial project.

SIMONE
Wait, don't go. Follow me, we'll find a peaceful place to bury his father and then we'll continue on our way. And we *will* find one. Quickly. In the next village then, the one at the bottom of the valley. But not here.

AMÉ
I'm not going back to any village unless it's to kill everyone. Everyone. This corpse – I look at it and I see all those who are going to meet the same end. I'm telling you, the enemies are our parents, so we shouldn't go back to ANY village at all! We should disembowel our parents and leave their bodies to rot in the sun and take off to go all over and blow everything up, break everything, burn everything. We'll round them up along a big wall, we'll line them up and we'll scream at them! We'll tell them that the evil they're done to us is worse than murder, we'll tell them that what they've taken from us is irreplaceable, they've killed the visions of our youth, of our most precious miracles. We'll tell them that they've taken away our playmates and that in their memory we'll put a crown of their bloody skulls on our playmates' tombs. Then we'll raise our guns to our parents, our guns, and without remorse: TaTaTaTaTaTaTaTaTaTaTaTaTaTaTaTaTa!

SIMONE
Amé, control your anger. It's huge and beautiful but keep it under control. Look. We're both here. For nights I dreamed of the day we would meet. The day has finally come, so have faith and let's not argue. Wilfrid is right to want a calm place to bury his father's body. Trust in what's right, Amé, even if you can't see it yet. It doesn't matter what you are, what you've done, it doesn't matter because all those nights you turned on your light to answer the call of my violin and now you're here. Have faith, Amé, and come with us.

— 29. Decomposition —

Blazing sun. Tremendous heat. In the middle of a road.

WILFRID
Guiromelan, help me. It's so heavy.

KNIGHT
Wilfrid, I can't come running anymore when you call. You're asking me to come to your aid for things I'm powerless against.

WILFRID
But you promised me, you swore you would always be there, remember, nothing is stronger than the dream that binds us forever!

KNIGHT
Nothing is stronger Wilfrid, I swear!

WILFRID
Well I don't find it very strong, if you really want to know. It's not helping me a whole lot!

KNIGHT
But what do you want me to do? I can't do anything, you're carrying your father and me, poor dream, I'm still wandering, I can't lift anything or carry anything at all!

WILFRID
What good are you then? Hey, dream, what use are you if you can't change the world, what good are you?

KNIGHT
Arthur, my king, told me to never believe in death, that true death only exists in the minds of the despairing, and I'm not despairing. I keep going, I keep walking here, on this sad elevation. I'm a knight, by God, and I will maintain my honour and my dignity, I won't bow my head, I won't take off my costume, I'll stay here, just being what I am, the invisible brother to a visible being.

SIMONE
Do you want us to stop for a while Wilfrid?

WILFRID
Good idea.

SIMONE
Does it keep descending like this for long?

AMÉ
To the bottom of the valley. Another three or four hours.

WILFRID
It's so hot!

SIMONE
Let's stop for a while!

The FATHER dabs at his face with a sponge dipped in green makeup.

WILFRID
Dad, what are you doing?

FATHER
Nothing, I'm rotting. What do you expect me to do? What else do you want a dead man to do other than decompose when he's been out in the broiling sun for five days? I'm rotting, in an attempt at authenticity, in an attempt to be plausible, I'm rotting, I'm turning a little green.

WILFRID
Wait a sec, I think I've found a temporary solution.

AMÉ
What are you doing?

WILFRID
I'm going to pour my after-shave on him, it'll change the smell a bit.

FATHER
If I were you, I'd worry about the mix of smells!

WILFRID
Play dead, I told you, and keep your mouth shut!

AMÉ
That's not a good idea. There's alcohol in it, it'll burn his face!

WILFRID
Maybe, but he won't smell as bad.

SIMONE
All right, let's go!

—— 30. Signals ——

On the road. WILFRID and the FATHER fall.

WILFRID
Amé would you mind carrying him a while?

AMÉ
I'll never touch your corpse.

SIMONE
I'll help you, Wilfrid

WILFRID
No, it has to be just one of us, otherwise we'll both be exhausted.

FATHER
Don't you think he looks a bit like your uncle Émile?

WILFRID
You're right, there's a strong resemblance.

SIMONE
It's getting dark, we'll stop here.

WILFRID
Good idea.

SIMONE
Look at the sky, there's the north star.

FATHER
Wilfrid, when you're young, people tell you so little about life that we spend the rest of our existence struggling to grasp what

we'd have had no trouble understanding as children. Death is so sad. Oh!! A mouse! Mousie, mousie, mousie, here little mousie.... Wilfrid, look, the mouse is alive and it came here, drawn by the living smell of death that I am, here little mousie, nibble my finger, eat my liver, my spleen! Oh, all these living things around me, that breathe, grow bigger, grow old! And me, dead, I'm giving off a stench that makes the stars shudder. And they're shuddering, they're certainly shuddering!

SIMONE
Listen! It's quiet, the dead of night. It's time! (*She shouts:*) "The time has come to make this one single effort!" "Here I am." "Here I am." "At the crossroads, we might meet the Other."

SIMONE plays her violin. Another instrument answers.

SIMONE
Do you hear?

WILFRID
A drum.

SIMONE
There's someone there!

SIMONE plays her violin. The other instrument answers.

I'll keep playing and the other person over there, will answer. With our music to guide us, we'll find each other.

—— 31. Sabbé ——

Encounter with SABBÉ. SABBÉ is laughing so hard he's in tears!

WILFRID
What's so funny!?

SABBÉ
Oh, it's hilarious! You're the one who was playing?

SIMONE
Yes.

SABBÉ laughs.

AMÉ
He's getting on my nerves!

SIMONE
What is it?!

SABBÉ
Nothing! Nothing! It's just that I pictured you as very fat. And here I was waiting for a fat girl to arrive, and now I'm looking at you and I can't stop laughing…

General giggling.

SABBÉ
My name is Sabbé. I saw you coming from far off.

AMÉ
What do you want?

SABBÉ
What do you mean what do I want?

AMÉ
Why are you here?

SABBÉ
That's a hell of a question! Why am I here and not somewhere else! If I'm here, it's because I'm not somewhere else! It's a lame explanation but I've nothing better to offer you. But what on earth – it really stinks around here.

WILFRID
Yes it stinks, it reeks to be perfectly honest!

SIMONE
It's his father's corpse.

SABBÉ
A corpse? Let me see! It's your father? It's your father's corpse?

WILFRID
Yes, why?

SABBÉ
That's funny! Two nights ago I managed to fall asleep for awhile and had a totally grotesque dream. I dreamt that I was with a few people in a strange place, and one of them was carrying a corpse, but a corpse that talked, had opinions, that argued, a corpse who was only playing dead… but the strangest part was the place, we were in an enclosed space, a huge place… we were confined to one end of the space, along a long wall and in the dark, there were people, people sitting and watching us.

AMÉ
Why did you come to meet us?

SABBÉ
Stop asking me so many questions, it's bugging me!

SIMONE
I'm Simone, this is Amé and this is Wilfrid. Amé is like you, he answered my calls. You answered them too.

SABBÉ
I answered, yes. I've been answering all your messages for a long time. In the village where I live, there are people who talk about you, they say you're fat and ugly, that you're stupid and mean. So I ended up imagining you with the most hideous face! People kept telling me you were depraved, yes, depraved, because you play your violin. So I found myself an instrument too and *I* started to play. But nobody called me depraved! It took me some time to understand, but now I know. No one called me depraved 'cause I'm tone deaf, but people kept saying to me: that girl up there is a whore – some of them even called you a whore. With her violin she leads people to their ruin! A whore! I said yeah, I went along and I laughed to myself because I knew who you were, I knew, the night showed me, I saw you through your bottles, your shouts, your music that reached me from so far away!

SIMONE
Do you want to leave?

SABBÉ
Leave! That's funny! Leave is a strange word. This country has

turned into a real joke, everyone wants to leave. Everyone. And you, you're looking for a place to bury your father.

WILFRID
And I guess there's no more room in your village?

SABBÉ
Here, all the villages are the same.

SIMONE
It's hopeless!

SABBÉ
So it's better to leave.

AMÉ
It's better, yes, so let's hurry and get the hell out of here.

SIMONE
Sabbé, do you want to come with us?

SABBÉ
I was sure you were going to ask me something like that.

SIMONE
Do you want to? First we're going to bury this body, then we'll keep going.

SABBÉ
I don't know. Maybe. To do what?

SIMONE
To tell stories.

SABBÉ
Stories. Our stories.

SIMONE
You're intelligent, Sabbé. Come with us.

SABBÉ
Maybe. I'll come if the corpse comes with us. If the corpse talks to me. If the corpse participates.

WILFRID
The corpse won't be going with you because the corpse is coming with me. I don't think we have anything to do together. It's true! You have a life that I'm not part of and I feel a bit like a booger in the soup, which must be the stupidest expression I know.

SABBÉ
You've got to be joking! Are you kidding! Look at you! You want to leave! You want to leave! Say something to him.

AMÉ
We have nothing to say to him, if he goes, he goes! He can do what he wants!

SIMONE
Wilfrid, stay, stay with us, we'll help you, we'll find a place!

WILFRID
I don't want anyone to help me anymore. Every time someone's helped me in this story I've ended up a bit deeper in shit, so I'm going to leave you alone with your stories and I'll just quietly deal with my own.

SIMONE
Wilfrid, I don't know what your presence here means, but I know there's no such thing as chance!

SABBÉ
So let's keep going together, we'll get to know each other a bit and later we'll have memories, things to talk about. Simone, let's go on.

AMÉ
Are you coming?

SABBÉ
I'm coming.

SIMONE
Are you prepared to leave everything behind to come?

SABBÉ
I'll leave everything behind.

SIMONE
We're going to tell people our stories, are you ready to tell yours?

SABBÉ
I have a very funny story, you'll see, you'll laugh your heads off.

SIMONE
Let's go then.

SABBÉ
Yes, let's go. Only we'll make a little detour through the village on the left. I have a friend I've never seen, but every night we laugh together. I hear him laugh, then I laugh. He hears me laugh, then he laughs. I think he'd be disappointed if I left without a word. And also maybe he'd be happy to come with us.

AMÉ
Afterwards, we'll climb up the other side of the mountain.

SIMONE
Yes, they say that from the summit you can see the ocean.

SABBÉ
Are you coming Wilfrid?

WILFRID
I'm coming. Leave me alone for a while, then I'll come join you.

WILFRID is alone with his FATHER's body.

—— 32. Prayer ——

WILFRID is alone. He talks to whoever or whatever might be listening.

WILFRID
Okay. I'm going to be clear now! Extremely clear! I know I've never believed in the existence of anything anywhere up there or down there or anywhere. And it's not because I'm saying what I'm saying that I've suddenly changed my mind! I don't believe! I don't believe. But just in case. In case there's someone, I'd like to ask that someone to do something for me, to do something and to do it fast. And I'm telling that someone in total good faith. On the

off-chance there's someone up there, if by any chance someone is listening, I'd like something easy to happen to me, I'd really like that! I'll even sign a contract with him. I promise, I really promise that whatever happens, I won't bury my father just anywhere, that I won't give in to despair and look for the quickest off ramp. I'll hang in there, right up until the body falls apart in my hands, I'm promising I-don't-know-who, something I don't even know exists, that I'll get my father's remains to a proper and restful place for his soul, but in return, in return, I want to know what I'm doing on this earth! I want to get to the bottom of it! Is that clear? And I don't want some evasive answer, I want an answer beyond any shadow of a doubt, is that clear? I think it's pretty clear!

—— 33. Rehearsal ——

Major fatigue all around.

SIMONE
Are you sure there's a village around here, Sabbé?

SABBÉ
I think so. Every night the laughter comes from over there.

AMÉ
There's absolutely nothing over there. The road doesn't even go there!

SABBÉ
There doesn't have to be a road for there to be a village. There's the river. I've known a lot of villages without roads.

AMÉ
I don't care. All I know is that there's no village around here.

SABBÉ
So he doesn't live in a village, but I have a friend who I laugh with every night and who lives around here.

SIMONE
Let's wait till night.

AMÉ
You buddy, I have a feeling we're gonna end up slugging each other.

SABBÉ
I like getting slugged.

AMÉ
And I like slugging.

SABBÉ
Won't we make a lovely pair.

SIMONE
Wilfrid, we'll wait here for a while.

AMÉ
Leave the body over there, it stinks!

WILFRID
I'll stay here, in the shade of the trees.

SIMONE
Sabbé, we want to go towards the big cities, towards the villages, you understand, we don't want to get lost in the forest. We want to go to the big town squares, stop and tell people our stories.

SABBÉ
They'll throw tomatoes at us.

AMÉ
It doesn't matter what they throw at us, we're going to go.

SABBÉ
I don't know. Maybe.

SIMONE
Maybe what?

SABBÉ
Maybe a lot of things. Maybe we have better things to do than go tell stories.

FATHER
Like maybe find me a place.

WILFRID
Maybe, yes, maybe find a place for my father.

AMÉ
But once we've found a place, what do we do?

SIMONE
We'll see. But we'll start with that. Find a place. If tonight your friend doesn't answer our calls, Sabbé, tomorrow morning we'll go up to the first tree that comes along, we'll lay the body down there, and we'll keep going towards the big cities, towards the sea.

WILFRID
As far as a place to bury my father, we'll see.

SABBÉ
Good idea, we'll see.

SIMONE
In the meantime, we'll figure out how to tell our stories to an audience. How. Let's say that we arrive, we sit down, we start talking.

AMÉ
What do you mean we arrive, we sit down and we start talking?

SIMONE
Let's try it.

AMÉ
What do you mean, let's try it?

SABBÉ
Yes, let's try it.

AMÉ
How?

SIMONE
Imagine we're in front of an audience.

AMÉ
But there's no one here except this river blocking our way.

SABBÉ
Imagine.

AMÉ
What do you mean, imagine.

WILFRID
Exactly, imagine, imagine, it's not that complicated! Take me, for example, I'm looking at my father's body and I imagine him talking.

FATHER
Hello sir. You're Amé, aren't you?

AMÉ
Yes, I'm Amé and I come from the Blue Village.

FATHER
I knew the Blue Village well. When I was little I used to play there, with the children. Maybe I knew your father. What's your father's name?

AMÉ
My father's dead.

FATHER
I'm dead too, but it's not that big a deal! Except for the smells, there aren't too many drawbacks. I'm still here, I still talk, I have opinions.

AMÉ
Yes but my father's dead and if by any chance he's still hanging around, the way you're hanging around, I don't think he'd really want to come and see me.

FATHER
And why not?

AMÉ
Because I'm the one who killed him.

FATHER
You killed your father!

AMÉ
Yes, I killed him. I killed him in the dark.

FATHER
Why on earth did you kill him?

AMÉ
Because I didn't recognize him. I didn't recognize my father's face. When I reached the crossroads, I saw a man covered in blood. I said to myself, what do we have here, just another piece of shit. I was returning from battle. I'd spent my night jumping up in the middle of the battlefield and shouting: "I'm Amé, it's me!" Men were proud to be slain by me. I took their weapons and threw their bodies to the dogs so that never, absolutely never, would their friends be able to bury them, and keep in this land a memory of their bodies, of their names. I was heading home just before dawn. I ran into this bastard, covered in other people's blood. I could see very well that this man in front of me was only wounded by other people's wounds. He took a step towards me, throwing up an arm. I fired. I emptied my gun into his red body, I looked at him and even then I didn't see a thing, didn't recognize a thing. I shoved his body aside and I left. When I got to the village people ran towards me, racing, racing, they ran to me to tell me that my father's body had just been found by a shepherd coming home with his sheep. My mother saw me from a distance and she started wailing and crying, she rushed into the abyss and she hanged herself.

KNIGHT
I'm suddenly painfully aware of every passing moment. God created me a child, and left me a child my entire life. Wilfrid, I shudder at the thought that one day you might no longer have need of me. I'm already less vital to you, less mighty, less indispensable, less of a saviour. Don't forget me Wilfrid, don't forget me.

AMÉ
So that's my story Simone. What good is it? What use? What use will it be for me to tell such a pathetic story to an audience?

SIMONE

So that the names aren't forgotten, Amé.

AMÉ

You say it's so the names aren't forgotten. But people don't need to remember that! They don't need to remember my father's name, my mother's name. They don't need to remember my name – especially not my name, we should trample it, forget it, burn my name... so why go tell people, why?

SIMONE

Things are bigger than we are, Amé. There's a current, a huge wave that rose up a long time ago and that's pulling us into a tide made of minutes, days, months, years, centuries, and we're part of it.... Just like our ancestors ten thousand years ago. They too were pulled by this enormous wave. So we have to be stronger than ourselves, do battle with ourselves, to leave the world our small testimony, so that the world will know what happened, so that they'll know that little Amé, one day, was blinded by his madness but that now, as he goes from town to town, he has turned back towards the light. With his friends. Sabbé, Simone, Wilfrid.

AMÉ

I'm nobody's friend.

SABBÉ

What a line.

SIMONE

The sky is growing dark. Night will be falling soon. Let's find a place to spend the night.

—— 34. Skidding and laughing ——

The whole film crew enters. They proceed to film in silence. WILFRID falls. A long burst of laughter in the distance.

SIMONE

Listen!

SABBÉ

It's him!

WILFRID
Who him?

SABBÉ
My friend.

AMÉ
A friend you've never seen.

SABBÉ
Unknown friends are the best.

The laughter rings out again in the distance. SABBÉ answers it. The laugh answers him.

SIMONE
He heard you.

SABBÉ
Let's laugh together, all together!

They laugh together. Nothing. They laugh together again. Nothing.

WILFRID
He's not answering anymore.

SIMONE
Maybe he's scared!

SABBÉ
Of what? Let's try again!

They all laugh together. Nothing. SABBÉ laughs alone. The laugh answers him. SABBÉ laughs all alone. The laugh answers him.

—— 35. Massi ——

MASSI smiles.

MASSI
My name is Massi. Last night, I heard music coming from very far away. I fell in love with it. Around here there are some old

peasants who live like recluses and who started a rumour about a young girl who could turn you into a pillar of salt with her violin. It was like they were talking about a witch who roamed the forest using her music to curse everyone who crossed her path. You can imagine the faces of the peasants when they heard you all – the music and the laughter… they were quaking in fear!

SIMONE
Consider yourself welcome among us, Massi. This is Sabbé who you laughed with every night.

MASSI
That was you?

SABBÉ
It was me.

MASSI laughs. SABBÉ laughs. They throw their arms around each other.

MASSI
Every time I heard your laugh reach across the valley to come and greet me, the stars became brighter, easier to read. I heard the laughter of a friend I knew nothing about and it would make me really happy. I'm happy now to see your face.

SABBÉ
I'm happy too. This is Simone, the girl with the violin, the one who left the village up high and who brought us together. The one who was the first to throw bottles in the river, the first to call out at the top of her lungs to make us brave enough to leave.

MASSI
We've heard a lot about you. Here, people say you don't exist, that you're only a legend.

SABBÉ
This is Amé. He followed Simone without hesitating. He's a great poet too, whose every utterance is full of meaning. And here's Wilfrid. He's carrying his father's body in search of a peaceful place to lay him to rest.

MASSI
I've brought a loaf of bread and a bottle of rose water. I told myself you must be hungry and thirsty. But tonight, with you,

I see and I feel so many things that this bread and this water take on a remarkable meaning.

SABBÉ
Give me the bread. It's been so long since I've seen any. Here, we'll eat, that's a good idea. Let's eat.

They eat the bread.

Do you know what they call people who break bread together?

WILFRID
What?

SABBÉ
"Bread Brothers." So in spite of ourselves, today we're all family.

MASSI
Let's drink now. I'll keep the leftover piece in my pocket.

SIMONE
So, Massi, do you want to come with us?

MASSI
Where are you going?

SIMONE
First, we want to find a place to bury the father, so that Wilfrid can go back home, then we'll continue towards the sea, to go from village to village to each tell our stories.

MASSI
I love stories. Yes, I'll follow you.

SIMONE
Are you ready to leave everything behind to follow us?

MASSI
I don't have much.

SIMONE
Your parents, your friends?

MASSI
My friends are gone. They've disappeared.

WILFRID
And your parents?

MASSI
My mother left a long time ago. I never knew my father.

AMÉ
Are you ready to tell your story, from town to town?

MASSI
Yes.

SABBÉ laughs. MASSI laughs. SABBÉ laughs. MASSI laughs. SABBÉ laughs. MASSI laughs.

—— 36. Isolation ——

WILFRID with the FATHER and the KNIGHT.

WILFRID
So who's going to tell my story?

FATHER
You're not from the same world, those kids have known war.

WILFRID
Well you know what, I'm starting to seriously envy them for having lived through a war, it gives them a legitimate reason to go talk to people. But nobody cares about me. A guy wants to bury his father, it's so ordinary! Hey, it's lucky that sometimes there are horrible things on the earth, otherwise we wouldn't know where to find stories. You don't believe me! Hey, Guiromelan, it's a good thing King Arthur got sick, otherwise your story would be a real bore.

KNIGHT
I am a knight by God–

WILFRID
Oh! Shut up! King Arthur is only a legend, a legend to make us

believe that that good old Arthur was a good King! But he wasn't any better or worse than any other, he shat, he pissed, and he died and he rotted all alone in his tomb! Go away, Knight, go away, you're right, I've stopped believing in the film, I don't believe in anything anymore, I don't believe anymore. And don't take it personally. But I'm getting tired of dragging a dream around with me so I'll feel less lonely!! I'm starting to find it pretty pathetic, I don't even have what it takes to give my father a proper burial. Look at him! And it's all your fault. You're always lurking around me, around my nights, around my body, around my mind.

KNIGHT

Wilfrid, I am a knight before God–

WILFRID

Shut up!

KNIGHT

And I was sent here by Morgan to endure the torments of the soul–

WILFRID

Will you shut your face–

KNIGHT

But my heart is a diamond and I won't bow before imbeciles, before the oafish, inept, lily-livered, hollowhearted and addle-brained! I won't exit your dream, I won't make you into a cold and brutish creature. You'll continue hallucinating in spite of yourself, you'll continue to dream no matter what, you'll continue your delirious ravings come hell or high water, you'll continue in spite of yourself, and if you refuse, you'll die.

WILFRID

I don't believe you! You don't exist! You're wearing a costume and you're speaking words someone else has put in your mouth! You don't exist, you don't exist! You don't exist, and if you'd never existed I'd be happier today!

KNIGHT

And you'd be stuck in your comfortable everyday existence, completely mired, your member protruding, in the confusion of bodies spraying your self-satisfied essence between some woman's thighs! For shame! I am a knight of God and I haven't invaded the soul of a blackguard! A cowardly shirker who stays at the rear of the ambush and tastes happiness at the cost of other people's blood! Retreat!

WILFRID

Go to hell!

THE KNIGHT

AhaaaaaaaaaaaaaaAhAAAAAAAAAA!

The KNIGHT kills WILFRID.

—— 37. Putrefaction ——

Morning. A huge jumble of bodies.

AMÉ

Have you seen the sky? The sun rose a few minutes ago and we're already sweltering! The day will be suffocating! We have to leave him here. We have to leave the body here, in the forest, under the first tree!

WILFRID

No.

AMÉ

What do you mean, no?

SABBÉ

He said no.

AMÉ

Where then?

SABBÉ

I don't know, but not just anywhere.

AMÉ

Tell me I'm dreaming, please, someone tell me this is a dream! You really want to carry a body that is seriously decomposing to I don't know where?

SABBÉ

Yes, why not?

AMÉ

You've got to be joking!

SABBÉ

I'm always joking. As a matter of fact, ever since I saw you, I've been laughing even more! My eyes are two different colours, I don't know whether you've noticed, and it helps me to see in four dimensions. The moment I saw your moronic little face, I immediately knew who I was dealing with! Right away! I know you, I know you well! Murderers like you, I've seen a lot of them everywhere! Everywhere! I'm happy to keep him, the corpse, because I think it's a beautiful thing, a corpse that has a head on its shoulders. That has all its arms, all its legs. I find it beautiful. The smell is nothing, actually, I like it, it's almost reassuring, it reminds me that the body's still here, not lost, not stolen, not burned. I was a son. My name is Sabbé, and my father – I feel like I'm seeing him! Simone, we're going to imagine we're in front of an audience. I'm standing and I'm telling my story. I'm saying: My name is Sabbé. My father died. Died isn't a strong enough word. My father was taken alive, fully alive! Soldiers took him away while we watched, my mother and I. Everyone was yelling, everyone was screaming! They took us to the playing field. They made my father get on his knees. In front of my mother. They laughed. My father cried. First they cut off his arms, then his legs. They forced us to watch, then, they finished by laughing as they sliced off his head. I started to laugh too. I laughed at my father's head when one of the soldiers shoved it into my hands. Then they grabbed the head and threw it on the ground and they played soccer with it. I laughed, I was laughing, my mother at my feet, I was laughing, I laughed… I didn't stop laughing…. Even before going to tell stories to anyone Simone, we have to bury this body. Amé, whether you like it or not, this corpse is the body of your father. Stand up, my friend, stand up straight. Open your eyes and recognize in him the father who disappeared, the father who was murdered, the father covered in blood. Recognize in him the father of all our pain. Let's go find him a place and let's bury him once and for all. We'll leave from there free, freer, free!

SIMONE

And we'll lay a stone, with the names of each of our fathers.

WILFRID

Where can we go?

SABBÉ

To the sea. Let's follow the river. We'll come to a place where it narrows a bit and that's where we'll cross.

SIMONE

Onward.

ROAD

— 38. Dreams and murmurs —

Dark night. The FATHER and the KNIGHT.

KNIGHT
Ah, Death!

FATHER
Ah, Dream!

KNIGHT
Where will we find the single thing that gives us peace?

FATHER
I'm telling you, knight, I'm telling you. We are nothing. What we seek is everything. Dead man's honour.

KNIGHT
Easily said, but not easily done, I tell you. Knight's honour.

FATHER
It worked. They're all asleep.

KNIGHT
It's so quiet all of a sudden.

FATHER
I guess a dead man talking to a dream isn't exactly deafening.

VOICE
Mira Abou-Casteldiniou, Mika Abou-Casteldiniou, Jean Abou-Casteldiniou, Charlotte Abou-Casteldiniou.

KNIGHT
Do you hear that?

FATHER
I hear it, yes

VOICE
Abiel Bakir and his wife Isabelle Bakir née Balaade. Their three children: Micha, Frida, Léna. Nabika Candika, Miro Candika,

Georges Digdanne, Antoinette Digdanne, Jean Digdanne, Alain Digdanne, Rita Digdanne, Roger Digdanne, Gilles Foudda, Micheline and Jacqueline Garba, Jean Ismert, Sarah Ismert, Miria Marinia, Billy Marinia, Christopher Marinia, Emmanuel Marinia, Manon Marinia, Joseph Marinia, Niham Marinia, David Nana, Liliane Nana, Claude Nana, Nayla Na, Naji Na…

KNIGHT
What should we do?

FATHER
What *can* we do? I'm dead and you don't exist!

VOICE
… Rima Ricou, Mathieu Ricou, Steve Ricou, Aline Saloum, Antoine Saloum, Lucie Saloum, Lucie Tanios, Chantal Tanios, Carole Tanios, Pascal Tanios, Caline Tanios, Abdo Tanios, Georges Tanios, Nelly Wajouda, Neel Wajouda, William Wajouda, Edwige Wajouda and Esther Wajouda.

KNIGHT
The voice is approaching.

FATHER
It's almost daybreak.

VOICE
And then the dead from the Stone Village. The entire Arkastalland family, Robert, Charles, Éric, the four babies, whose names no one remembers. Monsieur Laplante, who died in the arms of his actor son who used to step-dance in the village square. There's also the entire Bernika family, found under the rubble: Liba, Bénielle, Camil, Fred, Micho, Ekiel, Armand, Fourk, Ziad, Nouhar, Souhayla, Laure, Nazha, Sonia, and also the other Sonia, from the Sarkis family, and the one from the El Kamar family, Sonia El Kamar, who came from the Monastery-of-the-Moon village, found raped with her throat slit under the white stone. I'll remember all your names too as long as I need to, Sonia, Sonia, Sonia.

—— 39. Joséphine ——

A young woman is standing in the middle of the now awake group. She's carrying a large number of thick, heavy books.

JOSÉPHINE
Would anyone have a pencil?

SIMONE
A what?

JOSÉPHINE
A pencil! Mira Abou-Casteldiniou, Mika Abou-Casteldiniou, Jean Abou-Casteldiniou, Charlotte Abou-Casteldiniou.

SIMONE
A pencil!?

JOSÉPHINE
Yes, a pencil, please, it's quite urgent! Abiel Bakir and his wife Isabelle Bakir née Balaade. Their three children: Micha, Frida, Léna, Nabika Candika, Miro Candika. I've lost mine. It's stupid, it's so stupid! It was the last one I had! It's stupid. You can never plan carefully enough. Would anyone have a pencil I could borrow? *(SIMONE hands her a pencil.)* Thank you so much! You're saving my life! Believe me.

WILFRID
I have some paper too, if you want.

JOSÉPHINE
No, paper isn't a problem, there's plenty of paper. But the pencil, I swear, it was getting serious. I had to learn it all by heart, I couldn't sleep anymore, I was so afraid of forgetting everything.

SIMONE
Of forgetting what?

JOSÉPHINE
The names, all the names!

SIMONE
What names?

JOSÉPHINE
Wait, I'll free up my mind a little bit. Mira Abou-Casteldiniou, Mika Abou-Casteldiniou, Jean Abou-Casteldiniou, Charlotte Abou-Casteldiniou. Phew, that feels good! Abiel Bakir, Isabelle Bakir née Balaade, Micha, Frida, Léna. I've been following you for three days. Everywhere I went, people told me that some people had come and then gone again. Nabika Candika, Miro Candika, Georges Digdanne, Antoinette Digdanne, Jean Digdanne, Alain Digdanne, Rita Digdanne, Roger Digdanne, Gilles Foudda, Micheline and Jacqueline Garba, Jean Ismert, Sarah Ismert, Miria Marinia, Billy Marinia, Christopher Marinia, Emmanuel Marinia, Manon Marinia, Joseph Marinia, Niham Marinia…

SIMONE
What on earth are you doing?!

JOSÉPHINE
…Nayla Na, Naji Na… *(She continues quietly.)*

FATHER
All those names!

JOSÉPHINE
There! I'm telling you! Learning names by heart is really something. I'm hungry. You wouldn't have anything to eat?

MASSI
I saved a piece of bread. Here, you can have it.

JOSÉPHINE
Thanks!

SIMONE
But who are all those names?

JOSÉPHINE
People. They're names of people.

AMÉ
What people?

JOSÉPHINE
People. Just people. All kinds of people. People.

SIMONE
And what are you doing with all the names?

JOSÉPHINE
I write them down in a book, that's all.

AMÉ
That's all!?

JOSÉPHINE
Well, it's already quite a bit, believe me! It's not an easy thing to write down names on a sheet of paper.

SABBÉ
And what are these?

JOSÉPHINE
These? These are all the phone books from the big cities. It's a good thing there are phone books in the big cities, otherwise I'd still be at it. But in the smaller villages there aren't any phone books, so I had to do it by hand with the old people, I had to sit them down and make them recite the first and last names of all the people from their village. Old people aren't easy. They can be a bit annoying sometimes. Hard of hearing and losing their memory.

WILFRID
These are phone books from different cities?

JOSÉPHINE
Every city in the country. I picked up a phone book in each city, and in the larger villages. And then the smallest.

SIMONE
And now?

JOSÉPHINE
It's nerve-wracking. I think I've been everywhere. But with the war, who knows! There might be some tiny isolated villages nobody even knows about. I'm terrified of forgetting someone, hermits living in grottos, or recluses on the shores of hidden lakes. But it's inevitable! I'm sure I've missed people. And then the newborns. The ones who were born after I'd gone! What can I do? I don't know. I often asked pregnant women to tell me the names they were planning to give their child, but it isn't enough.

SIMONE
And what are you doing here now? Is there a village around here?

JOSÉPHINE
No. There's nothing left.

SIMONE
So...?

JOSÉPHINE
So I hurried to catch up with you. Yes. There are people here whose names I don't know because no one wanted to tell me.

SIMONE
Did you go by the High Village?

JOSÉPHINE
By the High Village, to the Blue Village, to the Village-at-the-Bottom-of-the-Valley, and even yesterday I was in an even more remote village than the one in the valley, where there are only a few starving people. It was in the High Village that an old man, a blind man, told me about you.

SIMONE
Ulrich!

JOSÉPHINE
Ulrich, that's right! He told me about a musician and a young man carrying his father's body all over to find a place to bury him. Simone and Wilfrid.

SIMONE
I'm Simone.

JOSÉPHINE
And this is Wilfrid. Ulrich told me you left to meet other people and bury this man's body. I thought that was wonderful, so I followed you. But at the blue village I met people who were furious. They told me that a young man had abandoned the village and everyone refused to give me his name to write down. The same thing happened in the village at the bottom of the valley. So I followed you. There are people here whose names I don't know.

SABBÉ
You've gone all over the country and you've collected everybody's names.

JOSÉPHINE
I'm not sure it's everyone. It's worrying me sick. But I think I've gotten the names of *nearly* everyone.

AMÉ
These phone books are from before the war.

JOSÉPHINE
I know. During the war, they stopped making phone books.

AMÉ
What use are phone books from 25 years ago?

JOSÉPHINE
All these names! Most of them left or died and no one knows where they are! So many people burned in this war, only their ashes are left, so their names…

SIMONE
And then, we lost the war. The country is lost. The country was conquered. And you've collected the names of the vanquished, of those that history will forget.

JOSÉPHINE
I started with the names of my parents, beside their name I wrote mine: Josephine, I'm Josephine. Those were the first names I wrote. Now I'm carrying all the names of all the inhabitants of my country. I'm missing three. Three that are here, among you. Ulrich told me about Simone, Wilfrid, and Thomas. There are only you three left. Who are you? And where are you from?

SABBÉ
I'm Sabbé and I'm from the Village of the Valley.

AMÉ
I'm Amé and I'm from the Blue Village.

MASSI
And my name is Massi and I'm from the lost village where you were yesterday.

JOSÉPHINE
Now I have all the names! Everybody!

SIMONE
My parents are in there!

AMÉ
And mine!

SABBÉ
My parents too.

MASSI
Mine must be in there too, but I couldn't tell you, I didn't know them. What about you, Wilfrid?

WILFRID
Me, well, I have no idea. I'd have to look in a phone book from the big city from before the war.

JOSÉPHINE
Here, take a look.

WILFRID looks through it.

WILFRID
Jeanne and Thomas.

SIMONE
You see, Wilfrid? You're from this country too, look, it's written here.

WILFRID
This really is my father's country.

MASSI
Look. These mountains. These trees, the sun and this sky, you come from here, just like us, and just like you, Wilfrid, we've lost our parents, so this father you're offering us, we'll all bury him together in a peaceful place.

WILFRID
I'm actually starting to believe that.

JOSÉPHINE
I'm staying with you. I've been alone for so long, all alone, I'd like to stay with you, walk with you. I haven't talked to people in so long.

SIMONE
Onward then.

JOSÉPHINE
Help me.

They help JOSÉPHINE carry her bags.

AMÉ
And now, the river.

WILFRID
The current is strong.

AMÉ
Too strong. We should have crossed higher up.

SABBÉ
Impossible. Higher up there are fields and the fields are all mined. We can only cross here.

SIMONE
Let's go!

—— 40. River ——

They cross the river.

SIMONE
Shall we keep going?

WILFRID
No. We almost drowned because of a corpse. It's not normal. It's absolutely ridiculous. And I have to say that now I'm exhausted. Really and truly. And we're going to stop here. End of discussion. We're going to dig a hole here, right here, and that's it. We're going to put the body down and it's over. And I'm going to go home. We've practically killed ourselves, I've done everything

possible to keep my promise, but now I've reached my limit. We're digging.

SABBÉ
You can dig if you want but *I'm* not digging.

SIMONE
Me neither.

JOSÉPHINE
I'm not digging either. I don't know why, but I know that I can't.

WILFRID
All right, take it easy. I wasn't trying to get you to dig with me, I'll dig the hole by myself!

SABBÉ
You can dig, buddy, but you'll be digging for nothing.

WILFRID
What do you mean?

SABBÉ
Because there's no question of you burying him here, anyway, I won't let you.

SIMONE
Me neither.

JOSÉPHINE
If Simone is against it, I am too.

WILFRID
What's the problem?

AMÉ
I'll help you. Don't listen to them.

SABBÉ
There's no problem, it's just that we don't think he should be buried here. We can't possibly bury him here. This place doesn't mean anything to anyone.

WILFRID
But what the hell difference does it make to you if I want to bury him here?

SABBÉ
It makes a hell of a difference, if you want to know!

AMÉ
Wilfrid, stop talking, just dig!

SIMONE
It *is*, in fact, your father's corpse and you can decide to bury him wherever you like; the truth is, we have no right to say a word. But Wilfrid, you agreed that each one of us would mark the name of their own father on the stone since we've all lost our parents.

SABBÉ
You agreed, didn't you?

WILFRID
Yes, Yes…

SABBÉ
You agreed to allow us to mourn for our own fathers, to grieve what none of us have been able to grieve.

MASSI
You agreed that in a way we would all become you and that you would become each one of us.

WILFRID
I hadn't seen it that way!

MASSI
That's the only way you can see it.

WILFRID
I'd like to, but I also don't think we'll ever find a place that's really the right place, a place like where we imagined we'd bury him. We nearly went and drowned! So let's bury him here before we lose our minds.

SIMONE
No. Exhaustion is nothing, and somewhere there's a still

unknown place to receive your father's body – *our* father's body. A place filled with light.

AMÉ
Here or somewhere else, it's the same thing.

SIMONE
It's not the same thing. Not here. Not here, Wilfrid.

AMÉ
But it won't make a difference!

SIMONE
Yes. It will.

WILFRID
What difference will it make?

SIMONE
If you still agree to play the game, because it's true, someone watching us, someone listening to us might say: "Their story… it's only a game." That's right, it's only a game, and if you want to play, you have to accept that we're also part of your story. So, according to the rules of the game, if you want to bury him here, we won't mark the names of our fathers, because we want our fathers to be laid to rest in a peaceful place, and not a site of fatigue. And this here is a site of fatigue because it's fatigue that's stopping you, that's making you change your mind.

AMÉ
But we don't care that they don't want to mark the names of their fathers. We don't care! Don't listen to them Wilfrid, and dig with me. Before night falls this carcass will be six feet under.

SABBÉ
You can bury him here and go back to wherever you want, but I'm telling you Wilfrid, the first night you're gone, I'll come back and dig him up and I'll carry him further away, towards a place that truly has meaning.

AMÉ
They're out of their heads! They're nuts! They're sick! Dig, Wilfrid, and let's go, let's get out of here! Forget about them! Let's leave them behind, I'm telling you! Dig, they can do

whatever they want, they can go dig up all the corpses on earth. They can't see straight anymore. Their brains are foggy, they've become obsessed, completely fixated, so crusted over with their delusion that they can't see the sacrilege of keeping a dead man among the living. Let's dig.

SIMONE

Amé, you're hardly one to talk about sacrilege, since there's no greater sacrilege than killing one's own father. As for this corpse, maybe you're in such a hurry to bury it because it reminds you too much of the father you murdered. With the corpse underground you're free to go back to your blindness.

AMÉ

You're the ones who are blind. *I* see clearly.

SIMONE

And yet you didn't recognize your father when he appeared before you at the crossroads the day you shot him, armed with your hate, your anger strapped over your shoulder.

AMÉ

He was standing in the sun. I couldn't see him properly. And there was so much blood on his body, in my eyes. I didn't recognize him. Today my eyes are clear.

SIMONE

That's a lie. The darkness that drowned your eyes can't be washed away with water. You were blind yesterday and you're still blind today. The light that blinded you is still blinding you today because you don't see that here, in this body, lies what might be your only chance of salvation.

AMÉ

Shut up right now!

SIMONE

Yell as much as you want, Amé, you can leave too, it won't change our convictions one bit. Onward.

They begin walking again.

MASSI

Are you coming, Amé?

AMÉ
What for? I'm all alone.

MASSI
I need you.

AMÉ
Nobody needs me. I shout, I yell, I get worked up, I cause trouble, I knock myself out – it takes all my strength to not blow my own face off. Nobody needs me, and I pretend I don't need anybody.

MASSI
Think whatever you like, Amé, but stay with us. Come on.

—— 41. Decrepitude and Dance ——

They're on the road.

FATHER
I didn't enjoy that little shower. It's shrivelled me up and what the current's done to my skin is far from flattering.

WILFRID
At least you don't smell as bad.

FATHER
That won't last. Soon, the dampness will work its way through my skin and all kinds of mould will join the party, and then I'll be completely oozing and crusty and disgusting.

WILFRID
You're rambling, Dad, I'm not even listening to you. You can thank them! If it wasn't for them, I'd have dumped you without thinking twice.

SIMONE
Listen, do you hear?

MASSI
Birds!

JOSÉPHINE
Tomorrow it will be the sea.

Night slowly falls.

FATHER
Knight, why does my son speak so harshly to me since we've arrived in my country? It was his idea, after all. I didn't ask anything of him.

KNIGHT
What can I tell you! I don't ask anything of him either. And I'm only here because he wanted me to be!

FATHER
What a situation!

KNIGHT
You're not kidding!

FATHER
So tell me, what does he dream about?

KNIGHT
Pfff! He's evasive in dreams, even in his fantasies. I don't know a thing.

FATHER
But yet you're at the heart of his most private thoughts! At night, when his eyes are closed, what dreams—or nightmares—haunt him?

KNIGHT
He sleeps badly, he doesn't dream, when he closes his eyes, it's the void.

FATHER
I don't know which of us has the more enviable situation.

KNIGHT
To be dead or to be a dream. What's the difference?

FATHER
No difference.

KNIGHT
So then?

FATHER
So nothing.

KNIGHT
Well.

FATHER
Yes, well. Meanwhile, I just keep rotting.

KNIGHT
The laws of nature are merciless.

FATHER
Why don't they leave me here, to simply bleach in the sunlight!

KNIGHT
Because the birds would peck out your eyes.

FATHER
Death isn't for the faint of heart.

KNIGHT
Neither is life!

FATHER
So, it's a no-win situation.

KNIGHT
You can say that again!

FATHER
This night actually reminds me of Mexico City. Let's not think about all this anymore, what do you say. Let's dance!

They dance.

—— 42. Insomnia ——

Night. As the music ends, we hear JOSÉPHINE'S voice.

JOSÉPHINE
The Baldanaade family, the Hakiniine family, Charbel, Yohanne,

the Gihanne family, Antoine, Samira, Émile, Mariamme, Clara, Kira, Anouk, the Kiralina family, Innèk, Bernard, Fred, the Champagne family, Jules, Hubert and the little king Arthur…

SIMONE
Josephine, are you all right?

JOSÉPHINE wakes with a start.

JOSÉPHINE
Yes, Yes, I'm fine! I'm sorry. I've learned so many names by heart that I can't fall asleep anymore without reciting a few.

SIMONE
Don't apologize, they were pretty names.

JOSÉPHINE
I have to say I don't know what a pretty name is anymore. But I know how sad it is when people move through life without anyone to call them by their name. Simone. Simone. Do you hear how it sounds? For so long I would repeat my own name as I walked because there was no one to say it. I was so afraid of forgetting it. Joséphine, Joséphine, Joséphine, Joséphine… I sometimes feel like a boat sailing an unknown sea in the dark, no lighthouse, no stars to guide me. These names, all these names, Simone, are my stars.

SIMONE
But what on earth are you going to do with all your phone books, Joséphine?

JOSÉPHINE
I don't know. I've been trying to find a solution for a long time. When I explain what I'm doing, people smile at me, they stroke my hair. Once a man fell to his knees when he saw the names of his family in one of my books, a woman in the Pomegranate Village hugged me tightly, not that long ago a child came to give me something to eat. In the Dark Village people waved goodbye till I was far away. Everyone encouraged me. Ulrich, the blind man, told me that I'm preserving a memory. He called me by a name I'd never heard before. He said to me: Safe travels, Antigone, I told him that my name was Joséphine, but he didn't seem to understand! Strange, they say that the blind have very acute hearing, but he waved to me again and he said: Safe travels,

Antigone. A strange man, that Ulrich. I really want to preserve the memory, but it's getting heavy, my hands are all blistered… so heavy. And I'll never be able to get rid of them. What could we do with them? You realize, the whole country's here! You can't just throw that away!

MASSI

All this time that you were walking along the road, your hands shredded by all this weight, what's kept you going? What's been going through your head?

JOSÉPHINE

I'll tell you my dream. My great dream. What I'd like, is in ten thousand years, for archeologists to find these phone books – and by finding them, they'll also find our names, they'll find the names of those who, ten thousand years earlier, were vanquished.

WILFRID

So where will you put them?

JOSÉPHINE

That's what I don't know. Where can I hide the phone books? Where can I hide them that they won't be stolen or lost…? Who can I entrust them to? Sometimes I say to myself that I'll keep them with me and later I'll hand them on to someone else, and so on, but they're so cumbersome! I don't know what to do with them! There's nowhere where I could be sure they wouldn't be plundered or burned. I'm worried sick! All these names, all these names… they're here… with me, with us, all these people are here, we can't just dump them, but I can't keep them with me forever.

WILFRID

It seems like we have the same problem!

SIMONE

Tomorrow, the sea.

MASSI

You can feel a hint of it already. With the wind rising up.

SIMONE

Joséphine, soothe us, with all these names, soothe our minds, please. Your presence here gives a sense of meaning to our coming together. You're showing us ourselves because you're giving us back our names.

WILFRID
Look up in the sky. There's the North Star.

JOSÉPHINE
Gabrielle Badhintère, Myriam Badhintère, Zacharie Badhintère, Guylaine Rouen, and then the concierge who died of fear in an asylum, Madame Déborah Lapointe. And of course her sister who disappeared, the sister with the blond look, Josée Boutin, monsieur Sami Youhbat, Éliane Youhbat, Mélanie and Souhayla Youhbat, Layal Leblanc and her brother Tristan who hung himself, Tristan Artaud.

SABBÉ
I've never seen the sea.

MASSI
Wilfrid, you've seen the sea, tell us what it's like.

WILFRID
The sea? It's mostly a lot of water.

MASSI
You've seen a lot of things.

WILFRID
I don't know.

MASSI
Wilfrid, tell us your story.

WILFRID
There was a guy who slept with his father because he was making love with a girl right at the moment his father died. And then, the guy ejaculates the ringing of the phone! It takes him by surprise. He answers. Someone tells him they've just found his father sitting on a bench, dead.

JOSÉPHINE
With your father dead, what did you do?

WILFRID
I went to see the Magistrate.

SIMONE
We have our story. A man seeks a place to bury his father's body. And through this story each of us will tell their own story. We'll tell our stories to people by saying and doing again what we've said and what we've done. We'll go out in public and we'll tell our stories.

MASSI
All we need now is to find the ending.

SIMONE
We'll find the ending when we find a place to bury the father.

JOSÉPHINE
And look, the fog is lifting, look!

SIMONE
The sea!

MASSI
The sea.

TIDELINE

— 43. Shore —

WILFRID
When I was little, my father used to tell me the story of a knight named Guiromelan. At night, after savagely battling his enemies, after decapitating the vulgar and uncouth, he would lay himself down in the sea. Each morning, the waves would carry him back to shore, carrying him back to life. The Knight Guiromelan knew that one morning, the sea would keep him in her embrace. She wouldn't toss him back up on the beach. That morning would be the day he'd be able to accept death. I know that my father isn't a knight, he's a dead corpse who's rotting before our eyes, but it doesn't matter, we're going to give him to the sea so that she can keep him with her. I'm going to wash his body, I'm going to wash his clothes, and when he's all clean, all handsome, we'll offer him to the waves. We're not going to bury him in the earth, we'll deliver him to the sea.

MASSI
We'll help you.

— 44. Undressing —

The film crew. Shooting.

DIRECTOR
Excellent! Let's set up the scene. For this scene I want us to feel that Wilfrid is baring his soul, and we're going to convey that through a very striking image that will very likely go down in the history of cinema. We're going to undress the father. We'll witness the moment Wilfrid, who has reached the burial site, actually begins to wash his father's body, a gripping image if there ever was one. Now stand here please. Touch ups on the father's make-up, his whole body, thank you. Here, start wide, let's see the waves thrashing wildly, as though the father's soul were rebelling at having to throw in the towel! Got it? You got it, right…? Right! Now, you, over here and then, we're going to create a mood by shooting all this in soft, diaphanous light, make the light diaphanous, got it?…

LIGHTING PERSON

Yes, yes, diaphanous, diaphanous…

DIRECTOR

Right. We're creating a kind of veil of modesty here in front of the father so that he can get undressed, then they'll take away his clothes to wash them in the sea. Stand by, first positions everyone…. You, Wilfrid, while this is going on, you're here, and as the scene unfolds, slowly, slowly, you place your hand on your father's shoulder, you turn your head slightly towards the sea, and you press your other hand to your forehead in a tragic gesture. Tragic, right…? All right, standing by…. Roll sound!

SOUND PERSON

Sound rolling.

CAMERA PERSON

Camera rolling.

SCRIPT SUPERVISOR

Undressing the father, take one.

DIRECTOR

Three, two one…! ACTION! Wilfrid, you undress your father, and it's as though you were revealing the hidden side of the moon! You're entering virgin territory! You're the first man to walk on the moon! Before you his withered skin is a cosmic landscape! Facing this vision, you can't help but think that this parched earth, this body, this flesh, this flab that's cold and darkened by decay, is the body, the flesh, the flab of your father. Your heart is pounding, you can't breathe, you're even wheezing, you almost pass out, because this body, this flesh, this flab, this parched earth, gave you life. Wilfrid, it takes every ounce of your will to not break down!

JOSÉPHINE

Wilfrid, are you all right?

WILFRID

Yes…

SIMONE

If you want, go for a walk on the beach, we'll wash your father's body.

WILFRID
No, I want to do it. Take his clothes, go wash his clothes, then spread them out to dry.

DIRECTOR
Excellent, place the corpse in a dramatic pose. Wilfrid, more than ever before, you're confronting death and you decide to look it square in the face, all alone.

WILFRID
Go on. I've seen the sea many times. All of you, go have a swim, leave me here by myself, I just need you to bring me some water so I can wash him.

JOSÉPHINE
I'll bring you some.

DIRECTOR
Stand by, we're prepping for the top of the scene.

WILFRID
Couldn't you leave too?

DIRECTOR
But I'm filming!

WILFRID
Exactly. Would you mind turning off your camera for a while?

DIRECTOR
What are you talking about! It's the most important moment of the film! You're all alone and you're washing your father's body, a gripping scene if there ever was one.

WILFRID
Exactly! I'd like to be gripped all alone if there ever was one!

DIRECTOR
Listen! I understand! Yes! You're giving me an idea! I'm going to shoot it but from a distance! That'll highlight the intimate nature of the scene, we'll see you at a distance, lost in the midst of this huge expanse. You'll become the man facing life confronting death. Excellent, excellent! I'm going to switch lenses. Go on, Wilfrid, never mind me, I don't exist.

JOSÉPHINE

I brought you some water. The others are having the time of their life swimming. They're washing the clothes. Even Amé's having fun.

WILFRID

And you, aren't you having fun?

JOSÉPHINE

No. I'm thinking about you. You've just found a place for your father. That's good. I almost think you're lucky.

WILFRID

Lucky?

JOSÉPHINE

I'm wondering what I'll do with all my phone books.

WILFRID

Stay with me. The two of us are kind of alike. Me with my father, you with your names. Stay with me. If you'd like to.

JOSÉPHINE

I'd like to.

—— 45. Recitative I ——

FATHER

Wilfrid, turn me to face the sea. *(WILFRID turns his FATHER. He starts to wash his FATHER. JOSÉPHINE is still.)* I can't see anything anymore, my eyes are shrivelled. Insects have eaten them.
I'm worried.
Facing this huge expanse that stretches out and disappears,
Way out there…
Who knows where!
I'm worried.
Wilfrid,
It's still not that long ago that I used to get up out of my chair, put my hat on my head and go out into the street with a spring in my step and the thought of walking all the way to the sea.
How painful the memory of such a simple gesture can become.
Putting your hat on your head.
Being cold.

Rubbing your hands together to warm them up.
Whipping into a crowded bistro and ordering a coffee, pretending to be absorbed in mysterious affairs.
Walking down the street.
Finding women beautiful.
Smelling their perfume.
Taking a bus
Hoping that one of them will sit down beside you.
And for a moment become your true love.
Then trying to seduce her without letting on.
Charming her
Making her laugh
Being mysterious.
And making her fall into your arms
By pretending your life is full of unsuspected suffering.
Saying adieu on a train station platform
And ending up alone again on the deck of a boat.
Striking up a conversation with a stranger.
Talking about the weather.
Being irresponsible.
Loafing around.
Doing nothing for sheer laziness.
Sleeping till noon.
Worrying about money.
Not knowing how you'll pay the rent.
Preparing a meal with friends.
Yelling at policemen,
Chatting with the butcher,
Being hungry
Being thirsty
Having a child
Staying calm
Staying alone
All alone
And dreaming
Dreaming
Being.

Wilfrid,
Wilfrid,
Is it sunny or cloudy?
My eyes have rotted in their sockets and no longer see a thing.
Is it day?
Is it night?

If it's night, then it's pitch black and not the slightest hint of the moon.
The water must be freezing.
Wilfrid,
I'm worried.
What are you going to do with my body?
Why did you choose to throw it into the sea, like throwing a condemned man overboard; carried off by the sea, just before he drowns, he can still make out, through the havoc of the waves, the others, the living, the ones who stayed on the ship of life and who keep going along their way.
I want to stay on earth.
I want to stay on land.
I don't want to drift away.
I don't want to be carried off at the whim of the waves.
A mangy dog,
A piece of flotsam,
Carried off any old way to any old place.
I don't want to disappear into that vastness.
I don't want to.
I don't want to be carried away
Torn apart
By ferocious fish
By boat propellers
By the reefs.
I don't want to.

—— 46. Doubling up and kiss ——

WILFRID washes his FATHER's arms and neck.

JOSÉPHINE

Sir…

FATHER

Yes, miss?

JOSÉPHINE

Would you be my father for a few moments?

FATHER

Very gladly, miss.

JOSÉPHINE
I waited for you for a long time, for you and Mama. Sitting outside the rubble of our home, I waited for you for a long time. But you never came.

FATHER
We were dead. Our shattered bodies against the wall.

JOSÉPHINE
The neighbours told me over and over.

FATHER
Everything burned. Everything. There was nothing left. Except for the phone book you were sitting on. Your dead mother wept to see you so alone, she said she'd have liked you to die with us. No matter how much I told her, over and over, that the dead can't weep, that the dead can't shed tears, it didn't stop her.

JOSÉPHINE
In the phone book, I looked for your name. When I saw it inscribed on the white page, with our phone number, then I really understood that you were both dead. I kept the phone book. It was all I had left of you. A name on a white page with a phone number.

FATHER
And now, Joséphine, what are you going to do? What will your life be now?

JOSÉPHINE
I don't know.

FATHER
You seem worried.

JOSÉPHINE
I have no idea what to do with my phone books. Do you know?

FATHER
I know that it isn't good to spend too much time with the dead and disappeared.

WILFRID
But when the dead and disappeared won't let go of you, what do you do?

FATHER
Who is this young man, Joséphine?

JOSÉPHINE
It's Wilfrid.

FATHER
What is he doing here with you at the edge of the sea?

JOSÉPHINE
He's washing his father's body. He's going to bury him here.

FATHER
Good afternoon. Wilfrid.

WILFRID
Hello, sir.

FATHER
Joséphine tells me your father is dead?

WILFRID
Yes, sir.

FATHER
I'm sorry. My sincere condolences. I can't thank you enough for allowing me to become her father for a few moments.

JOSÉPHINE
Oh no sir, *I* thank *you*.

FATHER
Don't mention it, miss. I hope I was a good father to you.

JOSÉPHINE
A very good father…

FATHER
Thank you, miss.

WILFRID is still washing his FATHER.

JOSÉPHINE
Wilfrid, what will you do after?

WILFRID
There's no after, Joséphine! After, I don't care!

JOSÉPHINE
You don't want to stay with us?

WILFRID
What for? I have nothing in common with you. You all have a reason to suffer, whereas I might as well go back to bed.

JOSÉPHINE
But the two of us are alike, you said so.

WILFRID
It doesn't mean anything. I don't count! I'm only a character. Someone who's in a dream world. But recently, a strange accident has thrown me here, into reality. It's pathetic for the dream to be held prisoner in a vulgar world.

JOSÉPHINE
But I'm a character swimming in reality too, Wilfrid! *(Slowly, she gets up. Very gently, she takes him in her arms. She kisses him.)* I'm only a character too.... Kiss me... a character given shape by life.... (*She kisses him.)* Kiss me.

WILFRID
Not here.

JOSÉPHINE
Here. The others are down there, far away, you can hear them laughing, you can hear them shouting, they've discovered the sea, they've discovered the crashing waves, the sky blending into the horizon, they're far away! Kiss me! *(She kisses him.)* Kiss me.

WILFRID
No! Not here! Not in front of him!

JOSÉPHINE
In front of him. In front of him, give me a sign of life, Wilfrid, and kiss me! You're here washing your father's body, steeped in the smells and secretions of death for so long, you're falling into his abyss, you're facing downward where there's only terror and darkness! Turn away from death and in your freefall turn your

face towards the edge of the abyss and look at me. Kiss me, Wilfrid, kiss me! I'm the light, kiss me, kiss me!

They kiss.

—— 47. Recitative II ——

While WILFRID and JOSÉPHINE kiss:

FATHER

My Odyssey is drawing to an end.
I'm returning to the harbour.
My country has led me to my country.
The road was long, but the reward is great.
I hear the rumbling of the waves
Interlacing all the way to the shore.
I hear the waves,
Panting, panting, panting, panting,
Towards the climax that will never come.
It's so good to be here.
To hear the sea rise up in anger,
Mad with desire,
Imagining she's the erotic pulse of the world turned towards the sky,
Then,
Plunging into her depths,
Losing yourself there,
Thrusting even deeper,
Where no one ever knew to go,
Going deeper deeper deeper and deeper still,
All the way to God's silence,
Then,
Just before drowning,
Whooshing up in wonder to the surface and beyond,
Towards the sky,
Towards the other depth,
The one that's infinite,
To then be pierced by the sun,
And fight against the wind,
And rise up with the waves,
And race along their crests
Then collapse, go to sleep and die, spent with love.

All this is over for me.
From now on,
I'll remain standing, my arms outstretched, not towards the horizon
But towards the infinite
That stretches high above, and down below,
That one can sense
In the North, South, East and West.
From now on I'll remain forever astonished,
Standing still,
Never able to go farther.
I so would have liked, while I was alive, to walk on water too.
To be able to keep going, continue along the road
And discover
What whales, dolphins, sharks and giant turtles experience
When they return to the surface.
All I can do is hope that my body,
Once thrown into the sea,
Will travel to those rocks they call reefs
That'll catch hold of me
And then,
Firmly anchored by my roots to the roots of the seaweed,
I'll become a friend to the mussels, the sea urchins, and starfish.
Because I don't want,
I don't want my body to drift away,
I don't want to drift away.
I don't want to.

How worried I am today.
The sea is there and I'm worried.
My soul seeks calm, but I can't find anything anymore.
Besides, there's nothing left to find.
There's nothing left
Especially in the face of this water.
There's no afterwards.
There's nothing else,
Why is there no moon tonight?
I'm worried.

— 48. The Horizon —

SIMONE, AMÉ, MASSI and SABBÉ return. They are soaked, happy. They spread the FATHER's clothes out on the sand.

SABBÉ

Wilfrid, look, we went swimming, the water was so warm, so, so clear! Even Amé couldn't resist and dipped his head into its foam! We baptized ourselves in the depths of its beauty. Our lives just changed with all this space that's flooded us. And you too, your life is changing, because by burying this body, we're about to turn the page, turn to a new day, turn to a new life. Tomorrow, at dawn, we'll start off again, we'll walk between tides, between the high and low watermarks along the shore to the next city, and then to the next country, then—why not—to the next continent. We'll go tell our stories to people who aren't like us, who don't live like us, and who think differently than us.

JOSÉPHINE

What are we going to do with the phone books?

SABBÉ

We'll keep them with us! We'll look after them, each of us taking a bag, our own bag, they'll stay with us until we find them a place.

MASSI

A place of their own.

SIMONE

We'll bury *them* too.

AMÉ

Oh no! Shit! Shit shit shit! We're not going to spend our lives looking for places to bury people! We're not undertakers!

MASSI

What's the matter?

AMÉ

I'm dying, for fuck's sake, from not having any future! Look at the horizon, I want to be like the horizon, I want to go towards it and by going towards it, go towards myself! I want to say things like tomorrow we'll do this, we'll do that! Tomorrow we'll build a house, tomorrow we'll return to our country, I want to say in ten centuries, I want to say: in a hundred years, I want to say: in ten years, I want to say: in ten months, in ten days, I want to say: in ten hours, in ten minutes, in a moment!

WILFRID

So for the moment, we'll start by laying to rest my father, who is willing to be yours. I asked him, he said he'd be happy to. Afterwards, we'll take care of the phone books. I've just washed my father's body. Here, now wash yours. I'm going to take a walk along the beach. There's something I have to settle with someone.

—— 49. Recitative III ——

WILFRID exits. The other five remain around the FATHER. They each take a turn washing him during the FATHER's recitative.

FATHER

Ah! If only I were a white bird above the sea.
I would fly far and dive into the folds of light.
I'd know true solitude,
The solitude of birds soaring up there
In the pitiless desert of immensity.
I'd finally know where the clouds go,
I'd see the great glaciers
Float together towards unknown places.
I'd be in the secret of the ancient things.

Who are you, circling around me?
Children of another custom
Of another country,
Of another continent

You with your eyes closed,
Don't lower your head,
I recognize you.
You're the one who killed me at the bend in the road.
Your hands full of blood,
Your heart is exhausted,
The world is exhausted,
Gotta end it
Amé,

Free yourself and open your eyes.
Because I'm telling you,
Like a wild dog, death bites.
It tears strips off our bodies.

You too, I recognize you.
You're the wide-eyed child.
When the men dropped my bloodied head into your child's hands
You didn't run away
You didn't scream
You stood there
Your eyes glued to the executioner.
Sabbé,
You didn't have the look of the humiliated
You didn't have the look of the tortured
Each of your eyes took on its own colour
And you remained
Cut off from yourself.
My head
In your hands
Cut off.
You have a diamond instead of a heart
But don't let anyone say after you've gone:
"There goes the child with the serious gaze
He wasn't generous, his heart remained closed."

It's your turn to approach
You who I long ago
Abandoned.
Neglected.
You who can maintain while watching the others:
"I'm the one who can't speak your words
because I didn't have a father."
Massi, come here, human child.
I kiss my laughing child and hug him tightly,
I hear the wind of the world whispering to us both,
I'm leaving for good for the opposite shore,
I'm leaving you, I'm leaving you,
And may your laughter embrace time.
We'll meet again, father and son,
We'll meet again, man and child.
Day is ending,
The light is falling,

Life is falling,
The tomb is calling…
I'm worried today, I'm worried.
I'm the boat whose lookout is shouting "Land."
Now it's my appointed time
To dock at the harbour.
But with no anchor to keep me from drifting,
My heart fills with terror.

—— 50. The Knight Guiromelan ——

WILFRID walks along the beach. He's joined by the KNIGHT Guiromelan.

KNIGHT
You summoned me, Wilfrid?

WILFRID
Yes.

KNIGHT
I know what you want to tell me.

WILFRID
I know you know.

KNIGHT
So there's no need to say it.

WILFRID
I need to say it.

KNIGHT
It's merely going to hurt me.

WILFRID
Too bad.

KNIGHT
It's over then?

WILFRID
Yes. It's over.

KNIGHT
You're grown up. Don't cry.

WILFRID
I'm not crying. It's just life stinging my eyes. Look at me, Guiromelan, look at me; as of today, no one will ever again call me their son! Today, there's a grief in me that I'd never imagined. Wherever I go, it will go, wherever I sleep, it will sleep. I want you to become invisible forever so that I can face it head on.

KNIGHT
King Arthur has just been cured then.

WILFRID
Yes, he washed his father's body with water from the holy grail. His heart is lighter. He's become more lucid.

KNIGHT
The wind is rising.

WILFRID
Later, when we give my father's body to the sea, you'll become the angel you've always been for me. Once you're invisible, I'll sense you better.

KNIGHT
So you want me to just lay down and die.

WILFRID
It's not that! What I'm telling you, knight, is that I want to become a man. Do you understand?

KNIGHT
We could become that man together.

WILFRID
No. I have to do it alone.

KNIGHT
But how will you manage without me?

WILFRID
I have no choice.

KNIGHT
I can't leave you all alone.

WILFRID
Don't worry. I've learned well what you've showed me. I've especially learned to die, which is the greatest lesson, but now, I have to learn the hard lessons of life and for that I have to be alone, without a net, without anything, it's my turn to step into the void without a phantom to hold my hand, but with a spirit in my heart. Be that spirit, be that angel on my road, that star my soul will be bound to. I no longer need to see you to believe in you. You see, I'm not asking you to leave, and I'm not trying to leave you either – on the contrary, I want you to live so deep inside me that we won't be able to see each other anymore. And later, when I die too, you'll come riding on your dragon to get me and we'll go slaloming between the stars laughing our faces off and killing the hairiest monsters in outer space.

KNIGHT
Wilfrid, even if I'm invisible, even if I'm pulled towards the depths of the sky, when your father sinks into the depths of the sea, even if it's the last time we see each other, I swear to you, I swear to you, I swear to you Wilfrid, that despite our hearts' disasters, we will ever be true to one another. My friendship for you is so deep that in spite of you I will remain your strength. Your friendship is so bright that you need only say the word and I, poor dream that I am, will set off towards you. Wilfrid, nothing is stronger than the dream that binds us forever.

WILFRID
It's the end of childhood, knight, and I'm going to miss you.

KNIGHT
Look up in the sky, birds dancing in a glorious light.

WILFRID
A diaphanous light.

KNIGHT
Yes. Make the light diaphanous. The time for the last shot has come.

— 51. Dressing —

WILFRID and the DIRECTOR join the others.

FATHER

I don't want to drift away!
I don't want to!
My body shredded by the waves.
Wilfrid!!
Don't cast me far from everything!
Don't abandon me to the current!
Don't throw me into the sea without an anchor!
I don't want to drift away.
I already told you!
I don't want to be dragged at the whim of the waves.
A mangy dog,
A piece of flotsam,
Carried off any old way to any old place.
I don't want to disappear into that huge expanse.
I don't want to.
I don't want to be carried off
Torn apart
By ferocious fish
By boat propellers
By the reefs.
I don't want to.
Stop!!
I don't want to be toyed with by the waves.
I'd rather you left me to rot in the sun, my bones slowly engulfed by the sand. I don't want to be dragged along any old way, I don't want to – or burn me instead.

SIMONE

We don't want to burn you.

FATHER

If you don't find a way to anchor me down under the sea, bury me, or leave me on the shore.

SABBÉ

There isn't a single rock anywhere on the beach, how do you want us to weigh you down?

FATHER
I don't know! You're alive, I'm dead! It's up to you to figure it out! It's up to you! To help me! I'm dead and I can't talk!

SIMONE
Poor dead man! You're frightened! How can we find something that could anchor you to the bottom!

JOSÉPHINE
I know. I have an anchor. A solid anchor. A heavy one.

SABBÉ
The names! The names from the country!

JOSÉPHINE
They're heavy enough to pull you to the bottom! Give him the bags.

SABBÉ
You want to throw them into the sea!

JOSÉPHINE
We were looking for a guardian and a place, we'll have the most faithful of guardians and the most secret of places! Here, this bag contains the names from the North region.

SIMONE
Here. In this one are the names of those who live in the East.

AMÉ
Take this. Mine contains all the names of those who live by the sea.

MASSI
Mine contains the names of those who live in the mountains.

WILFRID
And in mine are the names of the residents of the great plain.

SIMONE
Sabbé, give us your bag too!

JOSÉPHINE
Don't worry. I've protected them well. Down there they won't be damaged, and salt water protects, the sea preserves.

SABBÉ
Take this then! This bag contains all the names from the South region.

JOSÉPHINE
Take these, hang on to them tightly, they'll anchor you firmly to the soil of your country.

FATHER
Help me.

They help him carry the bags. They tie them around his waist.

Simone, be sure to keep throwing your bottles into the sea.

SIMONE
I will.

WILFRID
Down there, maybe you'll find a god or a devil, an angel or maybe nothing but fish. But *I* hope you'll find the soul of an old dog who'll come and sit by your side. You won't be dead anymore, you'll be a shepherd, because we're entrusting you with this flock. Be its guardian, and become then, once again and for all eternity, for us, the keeper of flocks.

—— 52. The Keeper of Flocks ——

The FATHER slowly walks into the sea.

FATHER
My soul is comforted,
Yet I'm suddenly racked by a great turmoil.
I'm heading off to the great quiet of the depths.
For playmates I'll have the names from my country.
There, among the fish, I'll be the keeper of flocks.
I'm leaving you behind
Forever orphans.
Even if you have to be a madman to agree to live,
I entrust to you the Earth,
I entrust to you life.
The waves are carrying me away,

The sea is swallowing me,
I'm going towards that country where we're all at home.
From now on I'll walk on water.
Wilfrid, Simone, Amé, Massi, Sabbé, Joséphine,
It's time to set off.
Walk along the roads,
Exhaust yourselves walking,
Leave before day breaks
Rage, and rage
At the end of roads,
At the end of cities,
At the end of countries,
At the end of joys,
At the end of time.
Right after loves and sorrows
Joys and tears,
Losses and laments
There is the tideline and the great sea,
The great sea
That carries everything away
And that's now taking me,
That's taking me, taking me, taking me,
Taking me, taking me, taking me
Taking me, taking me, taking me
Taking me, taking me, taking me
Taking me, taking me, taking me
Taking me…

The end.

Wajdi Mouawad is Lebanese in his childhood, French in his way of thinking and Québécois in his theatre. That's what happens when you spend your childhood in Beirut, your adolescence in Paris and then try to become an adult in Montreal.

Since graduating from the National Theatre School of Canada Wajdi Mouawad has written, adapted, translated and directed stage plays for audiences of all ages. He also founded the Théâtre Ô Parleur with Isabelle Leblanc, to celebrate language and ideas and send them travelling.

If Wajdi Mouawad had a punching bag he wouldn't write anymore.

Since January 2000, Wajdi Mouwad has been at the helm of Montreal's Théâtre de Quat'Sous. He has been programming seasons that voyage through the words of the shipwrecked.

Works published by Lémeac-Actes Sud: *Pacamambo, Rêves, Littoral, Les Mains d'Edwige au moment de la naissance, Alphonse.* In English translation: *Wedding Day at the Cro-magnons, Tideline, Alphonse* (Playwrights Canada Press).

—Estelle Savasta

Shelley Tepperman is a Toronto-born, Montreal-based dramaturg and translator with special interests in new play development and translation dramaturgy. She translates from French, Spanish and Italian, and has translated more than twenty-five plays for stage and radio. She has worked with theatres across the country, as well as with the Canadian Broadcasting Corporation, where she has been involved in developing and producing radio drama. She also writes for documentary television. This is her fourth collaboration with Wajdi Mouawad.